NAVIGATING THROUGH TRAUMA

Processing Your Emotional Wounding the Genesis Way.

DR ANNA DOS SANTOS

WESTBOW
PRESS®
A DIVISION OF THOMAS NELSON
& ZONDERVAN

This book is a work of non-fiction. Unless otherwise noted, the author and the publisher make no explicit guarantees as to the accuracy of the information contained in this book and in some cases, names of people and places have been altered to protect their privacy.

WestBow Press books may be ordered through booksellers or by contacting:

WestBow Press
A Division of Thomas Nelson & Zondervan
1663 Liberty Drive
Bloomington, IN 47403
www.westbowpress.com
844-714-3454

Because of the dynamic nature of the Internet, any web addresses or links contained in this book may have changed since publication and may no longer be valid. The views expressed in this work are solely those of the author and do not necessarily reflect the views of the publisher, and the publisher hereby disclaims any responsibility for them.

Any people depicted in stock imagery provided by Getty Images are models, and such images are being used for illustrative purposes only.
Certain stock imagery © Getty Images.

Scripture taken from the New King James Version® Copyright © 1982 by Thomas Nelson. Used by permission. All rights reserved.

ISBN: 979-8-3850-4305-7 (sc)
ISBN: 979-8-3850-4304-0 (e)

Library of Congress Control Number: 2025901929

Print information available on the last page.

WestBow Press rev. date: 02/21/2025

Endorsements from readers for the book.

"How often what we dreaded most overthrows the equilibrium of our lives and leaves us groping for a Hand to lead us through the resulting trauma! Anna LIVED it. She can therefore, with authority, give valuable guidelines from God's Word, from the stories of Job and Creation, together with creative artmaking directives – that silent language of the soul – to lead us back to a life of wholeness. Not only a book for counsellors, but for anyone who struggles with the result of trauma. Healing brings us into the 7th day of God's rest."

~Annatjie Laurie, Art Healing and Colour Interventions Counsellor.

"I am a dreamer. During my childhood, dreams accompanied me through a chaotic and difficult life. I also read. Books took me to other worlds and a place where I disappeared through the stories that comforted me and helped me escape. Initially, I thought Kahil Gibran could provide me with the answers to all my questions. Much later, I encountered Jesus. Unfortunately, I never had a mentor or spiritual leader who accompanied me toward a greater and fuller understanding of His full glory. This book is for people like me, seeking healing and renewal, hungry for a deeper relationship with God, even if they don't have someone to walk alongside them on their journey."

~Abraham Brits

"This book provides insights into the brokenness that happens because of trauma. Without the danger of re-traumatization, the emotionally wounded reader will get the opportunity to experience the love of the Lord when they apply biblical principles in combination with creative artmaking in a safe and non-threatening way. Even non-believers will benefit from engagement with the artmaking reflections to encounter wholeness."

~Willien Diedericks. Social Worker and Pastoral Therapist

CONTENTS

ACKNOWLEDGEMENTS

I first wish to thank my husband Desmond for his love, selfless care, prayers, and encouragement to complete this book. I also want to acknowledge Annatjie Laurie, who walked alongside me not only as a gifted art therapist and advisor but as a friend and a visionary who dreamed with me on how the Genesis approach can be implemented; and Willien Diedericks, whose trauma-informed pastoral therapeutic lens deeply informed my study about emotional wounding. My deep gratitude to Dr. Jim Lucas, my pastor, whose prayers and friendship mean a lot, particularly during the season when cancer derailed my journey to complete the book sooner. To my children and friends, thank you for believing in me. I love you.

ACKNOWLEDGMENTS

FOREWORD

This is not a book about why bad things happen to good people. While this is perhaps one of the most vital questions that seekers ask along their faith journey, this book is not about that. It asks and answers another important and related question that serious followers of Jesus must address. This is really a follow-up question to the one that wonders why a good God could allow bad things to happen. It is this: "How do we help those who experience the bad things and are left with the wounding that so often accompanies trauma?"

As a pastor and theologian for about 45 years, I have had a front-row seat in observing the pain and suffering that is an inevitable part of living in this world. You cannot really care for people without walking with them through the challenges that life throws at them. In fact, along the way, some of that trauma spills over onto the caregiver. An older veterinarian once told me that if you want to care for wounded animals, rest assured, you are going to get bit. Wounded people are apt to wound others. Pain and suffering are part of the human condition.

In his 1940 book *The Problem of Pain*, C.S. Lewis endeavoured to address that age-old question of why bad things happen. He famously postulates that one of the reasons God allows suffering is that pain unmasks evil. It is His way of waking up the world from all the distractions that hinder us from realizing that something is desperately wrong with the world. I wonder if that awakening might also apply to the Church and not just the world at large.

Perhaps God uses pain to wake us up to the needs and brokenness of the people around us. Might the Church at times need awakening to the needs of those who are among us and even outside our borders? It is one thing to recognize the presence of evil, it is quite another to be willing to do something about it. But to be like Jesus we must be to do as He did for those he encountered; who were broken and crushed by the harsh realities of life. This book is intended to help us in doing just that.

This book is helps us understand trauma. In one sense it is a wake-up call for the Church to take trauma seriously and apply Scripture to heal the wounded. We learn that trauma affects how we see ourselves and the world around us. It often challenges the very notion of safety, trust, and self-worth. Jesus has well-equipped the Church to address just these kinds of needs. Those of us who are his followers need to avail ourselves of the tools revealed in this book.

This book is a guide for those who have experienced trauma. It enables them to journey through their wounding experiences in order to arrive at wholeness. This book is full of Scripture because the Bible is not shy about describing the painful stories of its heroes. As Isaiah prophesied, even Jesus would be a man of sorrows, and familiar with suffering.

Art has been a means of expression, healing and connection for centuries. When traditional forms of communication fall short, colours, textures and shapes can supply what words cannot. This book uses the transformative power of art therapy and Scripture to deal with trauma. Art therapy provides an outlet to gently explore traumatic memories. It facilitates healing through creativity. By drawing, painting, sculpting, or scratching out stick figures, people express and reshape painful experiences, giving form to what was once formless, and moving toward empowerment and wholeness.

This book is for therapists who want to learn more about art therapy and obtain a practical guide to using art therapy to help move people to wholeness. There is lots of technical information here in the first chapters that will familiarize you with the history and place of trauma therapy in the psychological sciences. It is also for the curious who want to better understand trauma and its various effects upon people. The insightful case studies will illustrate the profound need for care and hope for those who suffer. But perhaps most of all, this book is for those who are dealing with their own trauma. It provides a step-by-step process toward healing using the creation events of the first chapter of Genesis to provide a framework. It demonstrates how story and sacred text, when coupled with artistic expression, can create a therapeutic environment where pain is honoured, resilience is cultivated, and a renewed sense of self can emerge.

Dr Jim Lucas
Founding Pastor: Christian Life Community Church, Abbotsford. Canada
Adjunct Faculty: Summit Pacific College and Seminary
Adjunct Faculty: TWU Global, MA in Leadership

ABOUT THE BOOK

Emotional Wounding is Knitted into the Fabric of Our Lives.

> *"What is the point of life when it doesn't make sense,*
> *when God blocks all the way to meaning? Instead of bread*
> *I get groans for my supper, then leave the table and vomit*
> *my anguish. The worst of my fears has come true, what*
> *I've dreaded most has happened. My repose is shattered,*
> *my peace destroyed. No rest for me, ever – death has*
> *invaded life.*
>
> Job 3:23-26. The Message

Speckled like a thin line, and crisscrossing through its different layers, the thread of traumatic experiences is knitted into the fabric of our human existence. Yes, like joy and moments of intense happiness, pain and suffering also permeate our lived experience and awareness. Nobody is exempt from it. The aftermath and havoc of a traumatic event can leave a person in a perpetual state of chaos and turmoil. The confusion of trauma reminds me of what the earth must have looked like before its new creation, *without form, and void; and darkness was on the face of the deep.* Most of us know that trauma is not only limited to what our eyes can see. Notably, the Christian identity is intertwined with another suffering too—namely, Jesus's sorrow on the cross. Debra van Deusen Hunsinger says, "Traumatic loss lies at the very heart of the Christian imagination. The souls of those who call themselves Christian are indelibly stamped with the unbearable sorrow of this man, Jesus."[1]

---

[1] Deborah Van Deusen Hunsinger, *Bearing the Unbearable. Trauma, Gospel, and Pastoral Care* (Grand Rapids, Michigan: William B Eerdmans Publishers Company, 2015), 1.

You might wonder why this book was written. The answer is simple. It is meant for people who have experienced trauma and want to know and understand more about it. They also want to know how trauma impacts them, and what they can do about it. They believe that the Bible provides guidelines for everyday living, also when emotional injuries and pain have invaded their lives. This does not mean that non-believers can't use the book. No, far from it. I am convinced that the information for the book, which was gleaned from clinical research and Scripture, carries within them basic and universal truths that can be applied by any person who has suffered trauma wounding. So, dear reader, if you are battling with the aftermath of unresolved issues because of a traumatic incident in your life, you are invited to participate and use the knowledge and principles related to the GENESIS approach to trauma treatment to be your chaperone when you process your trauma wounds prayerfully and creatively.

As a clinical counsellor and an art therapist, I have counselled trauma victims for the past 25 years. During this time, I have observed that emotional wounding does not only affect the person directly impacted by it, but the devastating effects go much deeper and wider because it adversely alters the lives of their loved ones and their communities too. This aligns with, and is in resonance with van Deusen who says, "Traumatic loss is ubiquitous…When it hits us personally, it changes our lives irrevocably… Unacknowledged and unhealed, trauma often leads to further violence, either against oneself or against others, and thus to more trauma."[2] The destructive consequence of trauma therefore collectively affects humanity. The question for the believer remains, how do we address this wounding in a compassionate, clinically-informed and also biblically sound way? Over the years, and because reading Scripture is one of my daily contemplative practices, where I accept the Bible as inspired by the Holy Spirit and foundational to my relationship with God, I began to incorporate stories from the Old Testament in storytelling when I was invited to facilitate art therapy workshops and presentations. These workshops were presented on different continents and with folks from all walks of life. It was delightful when I encountered

---

[2] Deborah Van Deusen Hunsinger, *Bearing the Unbearable. Trauma, Gospel, and Pastoral Care,* (Grand Rapids, Michigan: William B Eerdmans Publishers Company, 2015), 2.

no resistance from people when I introduced the source of these stories as coming from the Bible. I know it does not mean that it will always be the case. Not every person embraces Scripture the way believers do.

During the COVID-19 pandemic, I was assigned to develop and facilitate group art therapy programs and workshops for trauma victims in several local community agencies. Observing how people who have suffered traumatic experiences find themselves in a perpetual state of chaos, I knew that the treatment plan had to be trauma-focused to include safety measures which incorporate emotional regulation and grounding activities. It also had to be attachment and neuro-informed. Working on, and praying about directives to guide the treatment plan, the story about Creation in the book of Genesis repetitively introduced itself to me. Finally, I developed a seven-session trauma treatment program where I used principles derived from the Creation story to determine the sequence and the art directives people engaged with, to help process their trauma.

These trauma treatment programs and workshops were well received. Intrigued by Paul's notion that "all Scripture is inspired by God and profitable for teaching, for reproof, for correction, for training in righteousness; that the man of God may be adequate, equipped for every good work" (2 Timothy 3:16,17 [NKJ]), I wondered, what if the principles of the story of God's creative intervention in Genesis 1 and 2 could be directly applied for individuals to process their trauma stories effectively, even when they are on their own? Subsequently, the GENESIS approach for trauma treatment resulted.

How did I go about the development of the book? I was reminded that Christians are not exempt from trauma and when that happens, they need tools and ways to process their emotional suffering. By dovetailing and integrating the disciplines of theology and psychology to inform emotional, cognitive, psychosocial, and spiritual trauma processing, I utilized elements and principles derived from the seven days of Creation, in tandem with invitations for Lectio Divina reflections to develop therapeutic artmaking directives that they can follow to process their stories of pain and suffering. By revisiting the well-known Creation story differently, readers will experience how their painful life narrative can be altered and changed. They are encouraged to engage intentionally and reflectively with the trauma-informed therapeutic artmaking directives provided to them. While prayerfully meditating and reflecting on the story of Creation, these believers who encounter trauma wounding will experience how biblical principles in tandem with step-by-step therapeutic practices and reflective art-making can assist them in processing their trauma creatively.

The first chapters are intended for the reader wanting to know more about trauma and the different theories around it. Scaffolding towards an experimental inquiry to explore how a biblical-anchored art therapy approach can be adapted for trauma treatment, Chapter 2 investigates some concepts and ideas around trauma in a biblical context. In addition to that I explored a biblical perspective of psychological wounding and how it relates to trauma. The story of Job was helpful to do that. Utilizing Job's trauma story to extrapolate principles for a trauma treatment approach requires some theological considerations. Considering the delicate emotional state of a person who suffers from trauma and the subsequent emotional fragmentation they experience; we also need to contemplate the stages of how the treatment should be implemented for optimum memory processing and self-integration of the trauma story into our lives. Chapter 3 was dedicated to contextualizing trauma, how it occurs, how it impacts people and how it should be treated. In Chapter 4, I explored the underpinnings for a biblical approach to trauma treatment and looked at the identity formation of the believer from a narrative and phenomenological perspective. I also look at the role of the Holy Spirit. I am convinced that, without Holy Spirit's intervention and guidance during therapeutic interventions, treatment remains dimensionally singular and often only cognitive or emotionally driven. The ethical considerations for the directives used in the book are thus based on the premise that God as the Creator, through the Holy Spirit, can still intervene creatively and restore lives today.

Using artmaking to process trauma is foundational to the GENESIS approach for trauma processing. Chapter 5 is dedicated to introducing the reader to the history of art therapy and what it entails. The essence and value of the book are to be found in the book's last part. In these chapters, the theories around trauma, and how it impacts believers are fleshed out as Lectio Divina reflections and artmaking directives about the story of Creation. Here, believers battling the effects of trauma get the opportunity to process their trauma story creatively. Through prayerful contemplation of Scripture and meditation, combined with art-making directives, designed with effective trauma processing principles, the reader can make art and reflect on their pain story. This results in meaning-making and integration of the traumatic events which caused fragmentation of memories, personhood and self-identity. The end goal of these chapters is to assist readers in their desire to live restored lives, joyful in their calling, worship and contribution to life as redeemed children of God.

Limitations of the Book

When I developed the artmaking interventions for readers to engage with, I limited myself to creative therapeutic directives for people with undiagnosed but self-identified traumatic experiences who are suffering from long-term adverse emotions and physical symptoms because of trauma wounding. In psychological terms, these trauma injuries are defined by the American Psychological Association as "an emotional response to a terrible event like an accident, rape, or natural disaster. Immediately after the event, shock and denial are typical. Longer-term reactions include unpredictable emotions, flashbacks, strained relationships, and even physical symptoms like headaches or nausea." [3] I also acknowledge the effects of cumulative trauma on individuals and communities incurred after the Holocaust, currently in the Middle East, Ethiopia and Ukraine, mass murders, school shootings, or the generational trauma impact of the residential school policies of Canada and Australia. Because this book is intended for folks who self-identified their experiences as traumatic it is not intended to diagnose or assess for clinically diagnosed disorders as identified in the DSM-5-TR.

The book is subjective and context-dependent, and I acknowledge my positive biases as it relates to the Bible as the source for the meditations toward art-making directives and reflections. In addition, I am aware that readers who read a book about trauma and engage

---

[3] *"Trauma"* The American Psychological Association. Accessed on November 20, 2022. https://www.apa.org/topics/trauma.

with it will bring their biases to the reflections. They will also have their unique perspective or ideas about the story of Creation. However, because trauma is so pervasive, and since the Bible includes many more narratives to explore as they relate to the topic, I am hopeful this book will potentially stir people's curiosity to investigate other stories from the Bible to apply in all the domains and dimensions of their lives, and not only during traumatic or painful seasons.

CHAPTER

UNDERSTANDING TRAUMA: ITS CAUSES, IMPACT AND TREATMENT APPROACHES

INTRODUCTION

Ambiguous Grief

He came unannounced and took us by surprise.
His shadow lingered, loitered still.
We tiptoed over it and pretended that he was gone.
Some nights when darkness falls
he filters through the walls and crawls upon my bed.
Hungry for despair he licks my scar and snarls with
discontent
when I escape into my dreams his shadow opens yet
another door.

Anna Dos Santos

Unresolved trauma causes people to feel perpetually in a state of mourning. Grief has become the shadow that follows them everywhere. To work towards restoration of this deep wounding, we also need to understand how it happened and what it has done to us. To grasp the full impact of trauma we must therefore explore this phenomenon holistically. Research about trauma, its causes, and how to cope with traumatic issues is extensive, mainly because it is so pervasive. The word trauma "comes from the Greek (τραύμα), meaning wound [or injury], and it is the alteration of *trōma*; [that is] akin to the Greek *titrōskein* [which means] to wound, *tetrainein* [or] to pierce."[4] In its most singular definition, trauma can be understood as "significant distress or impairment in functioning that results from exposure to actual or threatened, serious injury or sexual violation."[5] In this chapter, I will probe into why trauma happens, its manifestation, impacts, and considerations for treatment. I will also glean some Biblical perspectives to inform this inquiry.

Recent research has brought us diverse opinions about the topic. Darryl Stephen sees psychological trauma as "A protective response, a survival mechanism in the face of unspeakable horror, affecting relationships with self, God, and others."[6] He concludes with a redemptive stance, suggesting that "traumatic ruptures expose both woundedness and hope, [because] it is grounded in the human capacity to transcend these traumatic ruptures of time, space, and community."[7] In contrast, Judith Herman identifies the person who experiences these traumatic ruptures as a victim: "Trauma ruptures one's sense of space, time, and relation, trapping the survivor in a continual, traumatic moment in which the survivor may feel helpless in the face of existential threat."[8] This was the case for Hannah who suffered for years after she faced death.

---

[4] Gerasimos Kolaitis & Miranda Olff (2017) Psychotraumatology in Greece, European Journal of Psychotraumatology,8:sup.4. Accessed on May 12, 2023. https://www.tandfonline.com/doi/full/10.1080/20008198.2017.1351757

[5] John N. Briere, Catherine Scott, *Principles of Trauma Therapy: A Guide to Symptoms, Evaluation, and Treatment.* 2nd Ed. DSM-5 Update (University of Southern California, Keck School of Medicine, 2015), 20.

[6] Darryl Stephen, "A Trauma-Informed Approach to Christian Ethics," *Journal of Feminist Studies in Religion (Indiana University Press* 39, no. 1 (March 1, 2023):156 -160.

[7] Ibid.,160.

[8] Judith Herman, Trauma and Recovery: The Aftermath of Violence—From Domestic Abuse to Political Terror, 2nd ed. (New York: Basic Books, 2015), 47.

THE IMPACT OF TRAUMA

*Hannah**⁹

During the Apartheid era in South Africa, Hannah, a spritely 55-year-old equestrian, lived with her husband on a smallholding near a settlement of unhappy factory workers. Riots were the order of the day. One late afternoon, when her husband was away, and after Hannah had settled the horses for the night, she heard the shouting of an angry mob of people. Looking through her window, she saw a crowd of angry protesters waving pangas in the air, running towards her house. Unable to get to her vehicle to flee away, she did the second-best thing, ran to her bathroom, and locked the door. Crawling in a fetal position in a corner behind the shower curtain under a heap of towels, she heard the mob running through her home, breaking and destroying everything they could. In the darkness, they did not distinguish her body behind the gray shower curtain, and she escaped their wrath. Hours later, and after what felt to her like an eternity, the police found Hannah, in a fetal position still hiding under the bundle of towels. Later, when Hannah could revisit the memory, she repeated the same sentence, over and over. "They wanted to kill me... They wanted to kill me..." In her mind, she was still stuck in that cold dark bathroom, waiting to be executed.

Hannah's trauma story is a typical example of how trauma ruptures a person's sense of space and safety, and how years later one critical incident can continue to haunt the victim. Even though Hannah regularly attended church and confessed to being a believer, she never felt safe anymore. Afternoons, when the sun was about to set, she continued to check whether the doors were locked and whether there was a place where she could hide 'should anything bad happen.' In addition to being suspicious of groups and crowds, eighteen months after the incident Hannah became very sick and felt compelled to sell all her horses. Even though she and her husband moved to another city, Hannah took years to recover from the trauma she experienced.

Summarizing trauma as " An inescapably stressful event that overwhelms people's coping mechanisms," Psychiatrist Bessel Van Der

---

⁹ Pseudonym

Kolk, deepens Judith Herman's understanding of the impact of trauma by clarifying the effect of trauma on the selfhood of people: "[these] overwhelming experiences affect our innermost sensations and our relationship to our physical reality – the core of who we are."[10] This means that trauma, at least temporarily, distorts the story we tell of our personhood and sense of self. Trauma also impacts society. Staci Haines, who examined trauma's social, political, and economic roots, sees trauma as "An experience or series of experiences and impacts from social conditions that can break or betray people's inherent need for safety, belonging and dignity."[11] In addition to the psychological and social wounding because of trauma, Peter Levine introduces the physiological dimension of trauma injury and advocates for an additional layer of treatment to address it. In acknowledgement of the multi-dimensional layers of trauma, he believes trauma healing must happen holistically and that "It requires a direct experience of the living, feeling, knowing organism." Levine explains,

"Traumatic symptoms are not caused by the "triggering" event itself. They stem from the frozen residue of energy that has not been resolved and discharged; this residue remains trapped in the nervous system where it can wreak havoc on our bodies and spirits. The long-term, alarming, debilitating, and often bizarre symptoms of PTSD develop when we cannot complete the process of moving in, through and out of the "immobility" or "freezing" state. However, we can thaw by initiating and encouraging our innate drive to return to a state of dynamic equilibrium."[12]

[10] Staci, K., Haines, *The Politics of Trauma: Somatics, Healing and Social Justice*, (Berkely: North Atlantic Books, 2019).
[11] Bessel Van Der Kolk, *The Body Keeps Score. Brain, Mind, and Body in the Healing of Trauma* (New York, Penguin Books, 2015), 21.
[12] Peter A. Levine, and Ann Frederick, *Waking the Tiger. Healing Trauma. The Innate Capacity to Transform Overwhelming Experiences.* (California: North Atlantic Books,1997), 18.

For him, 'thawing' from the effects of trauma happens when the body has fully processed the painful encounter to be incorporated into the human experience. If that happens, the person can live an adaptive, typical life again. This means that trauma processing can not be addressed through talk therapies only. Having ascertained that trauma leaves vast and disastrous multi-dimensional psychological and somatic damage in its wake, a linear approach to exploring its effects will not be adequate to address such a complex issue.

North American awareness about trauma, particularly post-traumatic stress, only intensified after the USA's involvement with the Vietnam War (1965 -1973) when veteran soldiers returned home from war. Since 1990 scientific investigation and research about trauma and its treatment have improved exponentially, even to incorporate brain imaging tools revealing what occurs inside the brains of those traumatized. Surveys about the influence of trauma on the population of the United States of America have indicated that more than half of adults in the general population have experienced at least one major trauma in their lives. Two researchers from California, Briere and Scott, believe that these surveys could have been limited in their findings and conclude that "Most people in Western society will experience one or more potentially traumatic events during their lives. Of these, a significant number will suffer lasting psychological distress, ranging from mild lingering anxiety to symptoms that interfere with almost all aspects of functioning."[13]

Briere elaborates and states that "[Where] threats to psychological integrity (for example, major losses and other very upsetting, but not physically harming events) are also included, this proportion would be even higher."[14] In addition to this, the U.S. Centers for Disease Control and Prevention reported in 2019 that "Sixty percent of adults in the USA disclosed having experienced at least one adverse childhood experience, and almost a quarter said they have endured three or more

---

[13] John N., Briere, and Catherine Scott. *Principles of Trauma Therapy: A Guide to Symptoms, Evaluation and Treatment.* 2nd ed. (Los Angeles: Sage Publications, 2015), 20.
[14] Elliot 1997; Kessler, Sonnega, Bromet, Hughes & Nelson, 1995; Norris, 1992 in John N Briere and Catherine Scott, *Principles of Trauma Therapy. A Guide to Symptoms, Evaluation, and Treatment,* 2nd ed. (Los Angeles: Sage Publications, 2013), 18.

adverse childhood experiences which have resulted in physical injury and psychological trauma." [15] When these traumatic events happen without any physical injury Briere asserted that "people who experience major threats to psychological integrity can suffer as much as those traumatized by physical injury or life threat."[16]

Indeed, traumatic impacts can occur without physical harm, although all trauma threatens relational safety and the ability to manage distress. Jarred was a prime example of this. Even though he was never abused or injured, witnessing how his mother was abused and threatened when he was a small child, caused him great emotional distress. Over the years the feeling of helplessness was imprinted in his memory and started to impact his behaviour. He began to drink excessively, and the effect of trauma threatened his ability to remain in relationships. This all happened, regardless of his confession that he was a Christian.

Jarred*[17]

Jarred, an attractive man in his mid-forties, managed his own business. He was divorced and battled to stay in relationships. As a teenager, he excelled in sports and succeeded in getting a scholarship at a prestigious college in the capital. He came to counselling because he was concerned about his drinking habits that cost him his relationship. When under pressure in an intimate relationship, he often becomes emotionally dysregulated and has recently threatened his partner with violence. He presented as remorseful, guilt-ridden and shame-filled. It was difficult for him to talk about himself. After a few weeks of counselling Jarred began to disclose memories of his unhappy childhood. One memory that

---

[15] "Studies of adverse childhood experiences (ACE) in the 1990s reported that more than a quarter of the middle-class, well-educated, and financially secure Americans who were surveyed were as children "often or very often hit... so hard that [they] had marks or were injured." In James S. MD Gordon, *The Transformation. Discovering Wholeness and Healing after Trauma* (New York: HarperOne, 2019), 2. And in Bruce D Perry and Oprah Winfrey, *What Happened to You? Conversations on Trauma, Resilience, and Healing* (New York: Flatiron Books, 2021),100.

[16] John N Briere and Catherine Scott, *Principles of Trauma Therapy. A Guide to Symptoms, Evaluation, and Treatment*, 2nd ed. (Los Angeles: Sage Publications, 2013),18.

[17] Pseudonym

haunted him was when he was six years old. He remembered his angry and drunk father, threatening to kill his mother at gunpoint. Jarred was sitting at the dining room table when he saw the gun in his dad's hand. He grabbed his younger sister by the hand and ran with her to his bedroom where they crawled under his bed. Unable and helpless to help his mom who was pleading for her life, he tried to keep his little sister quiet. It was now years later. Sobbing in his chair he spoke about the fear, guilt and shame he felt for not being able to protect his mother. All these memories were stored deeply in his subconsciousness and the residue of the trauma he suffered as a child spilled over into his relationships. Jarred believed that he had no right to be happy or fulfilled in any relationship and tried to drink his shame away. He felt helpless to change anything about himself, and he believed that history would repeat itself if he stayed in a relationship long enough.

Courtney Armstrong explains that "Trauma disrupts healthy attachment and impacts the brain's ability to regulate itself."[18] Like most traumatic encounters it results in chaos and disorder. Stripped from feeling secure and safe in their relationships, people are unable to sense where they fit in, and they feel helpless to do something about it. Experiencing trauma is also subjective, and each person encounters it uniquely. Bruce Perry explains it depends on the nature of the individual's unique stress response and the intensity of the response to the event, to be experienced as trauma.[19] Perry lists "genetic vulnerability, the developmental stage at which the trauma occurred, historical trauma, a family's history of trauma, and the buffering capacity of healthy relationships, family and community to understand how patterns of stress can influence a person's stress regulation of inability to regulate it."[20]

Bessel Van Der Kolk, who, after studying trauma for thirty years, suggests that traumatic events which happened to a person in the past, can still be interpreted by the body as ongoing experiences in the present. He says trauma's devastating effects leave an imprint on the mind, brain, and body, which has "Ongoing consequences for how the

---

[18] Courtney Armstrong, *Rethinking Trauma Treatment: Attachment, Memory Reconsolidation and Resilience.* (WW Norton & Company, 2019), xi.
[19] Bruce D Perry and Oprah Winfrey, *What Happened to You? Conversations on Trauma, Resilience, and Healing* (New York: Flatiron Books, 2021), 2.
[20] Ibid.,103-104.

human organism manages to survive in the present."[21] Judith Herman observed and said these sensations "Overwhelm the ordinary human adaptations of life to such an extent that the result of the psychological wounding can potentially affect a person's entire personhood and how they interact with life."[22] When a person has lost a sense of the story of their integrated self it becomes difficult to experience a collective narrative with others or God.

Trauma alters how memories are stored, what our memories are, and consequently, how we experience ourselves. Van Der Kolk believes that trauma changes not only how we think and what we think about, but also our capacity to think. He describes how some brain functions are compromised when trauma happens. A traumatized brain is a sad brain and can lead to depression and insomnia. Douwe Draaisma writes, "Depression and insomnia transform our autobiographical memory into a tale of woe; every unpleasant memory is linked to other unpleasant memories by an oppressive network of cross-references."[23] Additionally, brain scanning has shown that several brain parts shut down during and after a traumatic event, including the thalamus. This mid-brain structure assists us in filtering out things we do not need to learn, give attention to, or concentrate on. When the thalamus shuts down, it no longer acts as a gatekeeper of attention. This means the person does not know which sensory information is relevant and what can safely be ignored. Van Der Kolk explains that memories associated with trauma are disorganized and fundamentally different from the stories we tell about the past. People dissociate from their old narratives because, he says, "The different sensations that entered the brain during the trauma are not properly assembled into a story, a piece of autobiography."[24] This further means that what the individual perceived happened in the past

---

[21] Van Der Kolk, Bessel, *The Body Keeps Score. Brain, Mind, and Body in the Healing of Trauma* (New York, Penguin Books, 2015), 20.

[22] Judith Herman, *Trauma and Recovery. The Aftermath of Violence - From Domestic Abuse to Political Terror,* (New York: Basic Books, 2015), 33.

[23] Douwe Draaisma, *Why Life Speeds Up as You Get Older: How Memory Shapes Our Past,* trans. Arnold Pomerans and Erica Pomerans (Cambridge: Cambridge University Press, 2004),1.

[24] Van Der Kolk, Bessel. *The Body Keeps Score. Brain, Mind, and Body in the Healing of Trauma* (New York, Penguin Books, 2015), 196.

could be fundamentally different than how an event played out over time. It implies that the mind has reorganized the event or the sequence of what happened, based on what the person felt happened when the traumatic event took place. A prime example of all these combined trauma-related symptoms became evident when I started to work with Marci.

Marci*

Marci is a schoolteacher. When she showed up for her counselling session, she was in a wheelchair. A year ago, she was preparing for a marathon. Marci planned her runs early in the morning before the normal traffic started. On the morning of her accident, Marci's route took her through midtown. The sun shone brightly, and the air was filled with promise when she adjusted her stride to align with the traffic lights to prevent unnecessary stops on the way. Certain that she had the right of way, Marci ran over the green traffic light. What happened next is still not fully known. All that she remembers is that she woke up in the hospital, with a broken body. Afterwards, even though her body recovered slowly, Marci began to suffer from depression, and she lost all interest in life. Even though the spinal specialist says there is no reason for Marci not to walk, she has not been able to leave her wheelchair yet. She cannot remember anything that happened after the accident or the weeks when she was in the hospital. Marci finds it difficult to concentrate and states that she sometimes feels fragments of the memories about the incident returning, but she cannot piece her memories in a linear pattern. She is afraid to leave her home. Marci is frustrated with herself and angry most of the time.

These overwhelming experiences affect the traumatized person's innermost sensations and their relationship with their physical reality. Consequently, "a depersonalization or a split from the self [occurs]."[25]

---

[25] Van Der Kolk, et al. "Pain Perception and Endogenous Opioids in Post Traumatic Stress Disorder," *Psychopharmacology Bulletin 25* (1989), 117 -121.: "[T]he thalamus functions as a "cook" – a relay station that collects sensations from the ears, eyes, skin and integrates them [..]into our autobiographical memory. Breakdown in the thalamus explains why trauma is primarily remembered not as a story, a narrative with a beginning, middle and end, but as isolated sensory imprints: images, sounds, and physical sensations that are accompanied by intense emotions, usually terror and helplessness."

Gabor Maté elaborates on the anguish and desperation related to the fragmentation and dissociation of self by suggesting, "trauma causes us to disconnect from ourselves, our sense of value, and from the present moment."[26] After the traumatic experience has overwhelmed the person's psychological capabilities, a rupture of the person's narrative of the self takes place. According to Van Der Kolk, "These traumatic events cannot be integrated into the individual's memory, but instead become "stored as jagged fragments in the body and … the trauma affects not only those who are directly exposed to it but also those around them."[27] According to Townsend, memories that have escaped the fragmentation of the trauma continues to "linger and haunt the present, and painful memories can become burdensome, like heavy baggage. "[28] Indeed, according to Paul Wong, "The emotional baggage and the scars we carry can sap our energy and reduce our sense of well-being."[29] Trauma not only alienates how we relate with ourselves and the world we live in, but it also alienates people in their relationships with others and with God. Van Der Kolk says,

> "Trauma, whether it is the result of something done to you or something you have done, almost always makes it difficult to engage in intimate relationships…deep down many traumatized people are even more haunted by the shame they feel about what they themselves did or did not do under the circumstances. They despised themselves for how terrified, dependent, excited, or enraged they felt."[30]

[26] Maté, Gabor. On Compassionate Inquiry. Accessed January 22, 2022, https://medium.com/invisible-illness/trauma-expert-dr-gabor-mat%C3%A9-a42a6ce67726.

[27] Bessel Van Der Kolk, *The Body Keeps Score. Brain, Mind, and Body in the Healing of Trauma* (New York: Penguin Books, 2015),1.

[28] Tamara L. Townsend. *Memory and Identity in the Narratives of Soledad Puértolas : Constructing the Past and the Self.* Lanham, Maryland: Lexington Books, 2014. https://search-ebscohost-com.prov.idm.oclc.org/login.aspx?direct=true&db=nlebk&AN=846022&site=ehost-live., 23.

[29] Paul T.P. Wong, "The Processes of Adaptive Reminiscence," in *The Art and Science of Reminiscing: Theory, Research, Methods, and Applications* (Washington, D.C, Taylor and Francis, 1995),25.

[30] Tamara L. Townsend. *Memory and Identity in the Narratives of Soledad Puértolas : Constructing the Past and the Self.* Lanham, Maryland: Lexington Books, 2014. https://search-ebscohost-com.prov.idm.oclc.org/login.aspx?direct=true&db=nlebk&AN=846022&site=ehost-live., 13.

According to Van Der Kolk, "Being able to feel safe with other people is probably the single, most important aspect of mental health; safe connections are fundamental to meaningful and satisfying lives." [31] This aligns with Maslow's theory on the Hierarchy of Needs and Martin Luther King's premise that humans are all interrelated. Gabor Maté furthers this view believing that humans have a "connection with all that is."[32] Stripped of emotional safety, traumatized people find it difficult to trust or to avail themselves of relationships with other people or even with the Lord. How the body holds onto trauma has a role to play in this alienation. Shelly Rambo states, "Trauma is fully embodied yet beyond comprehension, rupturing relationships with self, others, and God." In addition, she explains that feeling perpetually unsafe adversely affects the body by overriding the brain's logical thought processes. When that happens, "the body experiences trauma in ways that escape cognitive functioning and awareness."[33]

TRAUMA RESPONSE IN THE BODY

In addition to the internal chaos, fragmentation of personhood, and the inability to engage with relationships, the autonomous and sympathetic nervous systems connecting the brain with the body allow the trauma residue to be stored not only in the psyche but also in the body. Van Der Kolk notes the body ultimately "keeps the score"[34] of the trauma and will eventually confirm the emotional and mental symptoms that the person endures because of the event. Elaborating on how trauma presents itself in the body, Peter Levine clarifies that when something is perceived as an inescapable or overwhelming threat to a person, the body has three responses: fight, flight, or immobility. This happens, he says, "Because

---

[31] Bessel Van Der Kolk, *The Body Keeps Score. Brain, Mind, and Body in the Healing of Trauma* (New York: Penguin Books, 2015), 81.

[32] Gabor Maté, *When the Body Says No. Exploring the Stress-Disease Connection* (John Wiley & Sons, 2003), 280.

[33] Sally Rambo, *Spirit and Trauma: A Theology of Remaining* (Louisville, KY: Westminster John Knox, 2010), 19, 21.

[34] Bessel Van Der Kolk, *The Body Keeps Score. Brain, Mind, and Body in the Healing of Trauma* (New York: Penguin Books, 2015).

the physiological mechanism that governs the primitive, instinctual parts of our brains and nervous system is not under our conscious control, [therefore] the immobility response happens involuntarily."[35]

Starting to work with Anita showed me just how much pain the body can endure after trauma has invaded a person's life.

Anita*[36]

Anita is the youngest of two siblings. According to her, they were a very close-knit family. As a teenager, Anita was groomed by and, at the age of 14, sexually molested by a youth worker at a church camp. Guilt-ridden, but convinced by the youth worker that he loved her, Anita never disclosed the abuse to her parents. Sworn to secrecy, the shame and guilt about the incident started to take its toll on her. Beginning first with invasive thoughts, Anita soon battled insomnia. Unable to eat and keep her food down, Anita later displayed signs of irritable bowel syndrome. Her grades started to fall, and she no longer wanted to participate in any activity at school. To date, Anita still battles having a sensitive stomach and can't enjoy food like her peers. Years after the sexual abuse Anita is still not able to trust anybody. She is cynical about her parents' faith and does not want to be in a close relationship with someone. She has no set sleep pattern and is chronically in pain even though her doctor can't seem to find any physical reason why she is always unwell.

Staci Haines explains that because the body "absorbs" the trauma, these responses are evidenced in the body. She cautions that therapists, working with traumatized people, should not neglect the fact that the body is deeply affected by, and responds to emotional injury. Haines says, "In Westernized cultural and economic systems, we fundamentally live within a disembodied set of social beliefs and practices. This means that we have learned to hold the body as an object separate from the self."[37]

[35] Levine, Peter A, and Ann Frederick. *Waking the Tiger. Healing Trauma. The Innate Capacity to Transform Overwhelming Experiences* (Berkeley, California: North Atlantic Books, 1997), 17.

[36] Pseudonym

[37] Haines, Staci, K., The Politics of Trauma: Somatics, Healing and Social Justice, (Berkely: North Atlantic Books, 2019). 19.

INTERGENERATIONAL TRAUMA

Steven Levine describes the recurring effect of trauma in a person's life. "History repeats itself. For victims of trauma, the repetition seems endless. They experience themselves as reliving the traumatic experience again and again. The repetition comes against their will, insisting its way into awareness and dominating the field of consciousness, thereby inhibiting other possibilities of thought and action. Trauma never gives up."[38] The effects of severe trauma, described as combined and cumulative psychological wounding, can manifest even generations after the traumatic incident(s) occurred to impact our collective humanity. Intergenerational trauma research studies have shown interesting results.[39] These studies include the Holocaust, Intergenerational trauma in Black Families in North America, the Canadian Residential Schools and Brent Bezo and Stephania Maggi's study about the Ukrainian Holodomor genocide of 1932 to 1933. They have concluded that collective trauma continues to impact survivors, their adult children, and grandchildren. "Specifically, two superordinate themes were identified as stemming from the genocide: (i) emotions and inner states, and (ii) trauma-based coping strategies," affecting entire communities and nations.[40] These findings have subsequently also impacted the study of human genetics where we now see that,

> "The emerging field of epigenetics postulates that social
> experiences, including familial ones, result in epigenetic
> changes that affect an individual's genetic expression,
> in-utero, during early development, and throughout
> the life course. This field further hypothesizes that

[38] Stephen K., Levine, *Trauma, Tragedy, Therapy. The Arts and Human Suffering* (Jessica Kingsley Publishers, London, 2009), 65.

[39] Isobel S, McCloughen A, Goodyear M, Foster K. Intergenerational Trauma and Its Relationship to Mental Health Care: A Qualitative Inquiry. Community Ment Health J. 2021 May;57(4):631-643. https://doi: 10.1007/s10597-020-00698-1. Epub 2020 Aug 17. PMID: 32804293.

[40] Brent Bezo & Stefania Maggi, 2015. "Living in "survival mode:" Intergenerational transmission of trauma from the Holodomor genocide of 1932~1933 in Ukraine. *Social Science & Medicine*, No.134, 87-94. 0277-9536. Accessed May 2023. https://doi.org/10.1016/j.socscimed.2015.04.009T.

epigenetic changes are heritable and "may serve as a cellular memory" of human experiences that also shape the neurodevelopment, behaviours, and the health and well-being of future generations. In the context of intergenerational transmission of trauma, epigenetics may provide a framework to understand how survivor families are affected by complex transgenerational trajectories, stemming from their experiences with collective trauma." [41]

The intergenerational trajectory of trauma has a collective impact on certain population groups. Of note in Canada, the indigenous peoples of Canada suffered because of the Residential school system created through colonialization. The emotional damage caused to the children in Gaza during the 2024 war will most probably cause intergenerational trauma to the Palestinian people for generations to come.

IN-UTERO TRAUMA EQUATES TO SPIRITUAL WOUNDEDNESS

In addition to the reality that trauma can cause epigenetic changes at the cellular level even for generations afterwards, I am convinced that when a pregnant woman experiences severe trauma, more than the mother's trauma wounding, the trauma experience can also result in severe in-utero spirit wounding to the baby in the womb. Talking to hundreds of people whose mothers experienced traumatic critical incidents before the baby's birth, and seeing the impact the trauma caused on the selfhood and identity of the person in front of me, have confirmed to me that in-utero wounding results in severe spiritual wounding. They often experience a disconnect between what they think, feel and do. They are disconnected from their body, others and God. Or they are stuck in a state of mind that they can't escape.

---

[41] F.A. Champagne, Early Adversity and Developmental Outcomes: Interaction Between Genetics, Epigenetics, and Social Experiences Across the Life Span. Perspect Psychol Sci. 2010 Sep;5(5):564-74. https://doi:10.1177/1745691610383494. PMID: 26162197.on humanity.

People often say they have been anxious for as long 'as they remember.' Or they are afraid without knowing why. To be fearful or filled with anxiety all the time is not God's plan or design for humanity. From Scripture, we know that anxiety or fear does not come from the Lord, "For God hath not given us a spirit of fear; but of power, and of love, and of a sound mind" (II Timothy 1:8 KJV). Fear originates in evil and should be addressed, particularly when a person suffers because of in-utero trauma. By acknowledging the multi-dimensional levels of our existence and the fragmentation that trauma causes, spiritual wounding can be addressed effectively as well. That is a holistic trauma treatment approach.

A THEORETICAL PERSPECTIVE ON TRAUMA

Because trauma was so rampant after the Vietnam War, psychiatrists and psychologists continued their research and eventually identified trauma around critical incidents as post-traumatic stress. During the mid-1980s, *Post Traumatic Stress Disorder*, abbreviately known as PTSD [42], was finally classified as a stress disorder. This mental health disorder, endured by hundreds of thousands of people, is currently

---

[42] "*Posttraumatic Stress Disorder Diagnostic Features:* The essential feature of posttraumatic stress disorder (PTSD) is the development of characteristic symptoms following exposure to one or more traumatic events. The clinical presentation of PTSD varies. In some individuals, fear-based reexperiencing, emotional, and behavioural symptoms may predominate. In others, anhedonic or dysphoric mood states and negative cognitions may be most prominent, while in yet others, dissociative symptoms predominate. Finally, some individuals exhibit combinations of these symptom patterns....The traumatic events in Criterion A all involve actual or threatened death, serious injury, or sexual violence in some way but differ in how the individual is exposed to them, which can be through directly experiencing the traumatic event,...witnessing in person the event as it occurred to others,...learning that the event occurred to a family member or a close friend,..., or indirect exposure in the course of occupational duties, through being exposed to grotesque details of and event ....The disorder may be especially severe or long-lasting when the stressor is interpersonal and intentional (e.g. torture, sexual violence)." American Psychiatric Association, *Diagnostic Statistical Manual of Mental Disorders Fifth Edition Text Revision*, DSM-5-TR. (American Psychiatric Association Publishing, Washington, DC. 2022), 305.

extensively catalogued in a comprehensive diagnostic tool, the "DSM-5-TR,"[43] which is used to identify and diagnose mental health disorders. It serves as a resource for diagnosing mental health-related conditions from a Western lens and can be seen as a catalogue of traumatic impacts. Today trauma strongly influences stress disorders in the psychological landscape. People who experience post-traumatic stress never feel safe. Consequently, this perpetuates further insecurity, fueling the trauma cycle to keep them in a debilitative state of chronic emotional pain.

As we have learned from Stephen Porges's Polyvagal theory, there are several good reasons why people need to experience safety. The first reason is biological. At birth and thereafter babies need protection and only thrive when they feel safe. Secondly, people are innately inter-relational. "If they encounter extensive isolation from others, it is experienced as abandonment which constitutes trauma."[44] Thirdly, and particularly during times of great vulnerability, "nested within our need for safety to enable specific biological functions, are the expression of social behaviour and the regulation of emotions."[45] Porges's theory emphasizes that "evolution provides an organizing principle to identify neural circuits that promoted social behaviour and two classes of defensive strategies, mobilizing associated with fighting or fleeing and immobilization associated with hiding or

[43] American Psychiatric Association, *Diagnostic Statistical Manual of Mental Disorders Fifth Edition Text Revision,* DSM-5-TR. (American Psychiatric Association Publishing, Washington, DC. 2022).
[44] Studies on children adopted from orphanages in Eastern Europe show that institutionalization has a strong negative effect on developmental outcomes and that children with a history of institutionalization are more likely to exhibit emotional, behavioral, and relational problems (e.g., severe antisocial behavior and aggression towards others, disturbances of attachment). Following multiple traumatic experiences in institutions, including physical or sexual abuse, some children exhibit post traumatic stress symptoms and self-harming behaviors and report depressive symptoms. Children who grow up in institutions also have limited life opportunities as adults, struggle to adjust to society, and are more likely to develop mental illness or substance use addiction In Leyla, Ismayilova, Emily Claypool, and Emma Heidorn. "Trauma of Separation: The Social and Emotional Impact of Institutionalization on Children in a Post-Soviet Country." *BMC Public Health* 23, no. 1 (February 20, 2023): 1–14. https://doi:10.1186/s12889-023-15275-w.
[45] Stephen W., Porges, W. *The Pocket Guide to the Polyvagal Theory. The Transformative Power of Feeling Safe.* (New York & London: W.W. Norton & Company, 2017), 46.

feigning death." [46] It follows that, if safety needs are not met through perceived danger and subsequent trauma, people can experience dysregulated emotional states. When a critical event happens the person can either respond in a heightened state of arousal, which is experienced as hyper-activation to protect the self, or instead, they can dissociate through a state of hypo-arousal characterized by lack of engagement with internal and external realities. When the dorsal and ventral vagus nerves are activated, people can fluctuate between hypo- or hyper-aroused states. It results in a roller coaster of emotions with subsequent mental 'disorganization' and chaotic thoughts. This is also known as the fight/flight response.

To visually explain how a person's entire personhood is affected by trauma, I have drawn a diagram informed by the symptoms of post-traumatic stress. The diagram indicates how trauma invades and impacts a person's life to present as a triangle of multi-dimensional pain. From it, we can gather how the inflicted person's entire consciousness is dominated by intrusive psychological wounding which affects their physiology as well as their behaviour. Even though the diagram below provides an extensive list of trauma symptoms when just a few of these symptoms happen simultaneously, or at intervals, it can have a devastating impact on the individual's life. Based on Porges's explanation of how the neural circuits in the brain respond during and after a trauma event, we can now understand how people's memories can become fragmented. At the time of the critical incident when they no longer feel safe, and they feel helpless to intervene, the autonomous nervous system will transmit this despair at the cellular level to the body and its organs, where it is stored. When the experience of disintegration threatens an individual's entire personhood and they do not get the opportunity to process it cognitively, emotionally, spiritually, and somatically, the residue of the trauma will linger and manifest itself again whenever the person is reminded of the experience or emotionally triggered by something related to the traumatic encounter (see fig. 1).

---

[46] Ibid., 46.

The Trauma Pain Triangle

FIGURE 1

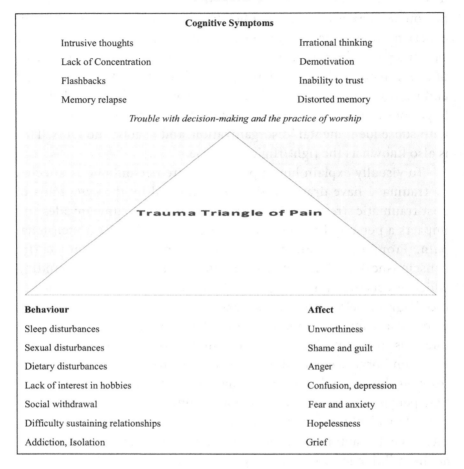

Cognitive Symptoms

Intrusive thoughts	Irrational thinking
Lack of Concentration	Demotivation
Flashbacks	Inability to trust
Memory relapse	Distorted memory

Trouble with decision-making and the practice of worship

Trauma Triangle of Pain

Behaviour

Sleep disturbances	**Affect**
Sexual disturbances	Unworthiness
Dietary disturbances	Shame and guilt
Lack of interest in hobbies	Anger
Social withdrawal	Confusion, depression
Difficulty sustaining relationships	Fear and anxiety
Addiction, Isolation	Hopelessness
	Grief

If trauma memories are not adequately addressed and processed, I propose this triangle of pain continues to disturb the person with multidimensional adverse symptoms as listed in the diagram. Without full integration of the trauma, re-engagement with life is hampered. When viewed from this triangular perspective, it becomes clear that untreated trauma dramatically alters and changes people's life trajectories. Not only does it change the person's present, but the pain and suffering that affect their emotions and cognition invade every facet of their existence and rob them of joy and hope for healthy engagement with life in the future as well. Making sense of trauma from an existential perspective, Stephen Levine suggests that "trauma, memory and imagination are united in our understanding and in our way of being. How we remember the past and imagine the future affects how we live in the present …Trauma fragments experience and prevents any totalization into a whole. In so doing, it robs suffering of its meaning. Trauma does not mean anything; it just *is*."[47]

There are different trauma types. Their impact intersects with one another. Following is a diagram of what that looks like. These trauma types are derived from information obtained from the DSM-5-TR, research of Briere and Scott, and Bessel Van Der Kolk; The trauma categories are a credit to the works of Briere and Scott and Malchiodi (see table 1).[48] Most critical incidents, and how people process them, have the potential to result in some form or type of trauma. Schematically these types can be categorized and summarized as follows, (see fig. 2):

FIGURE 2

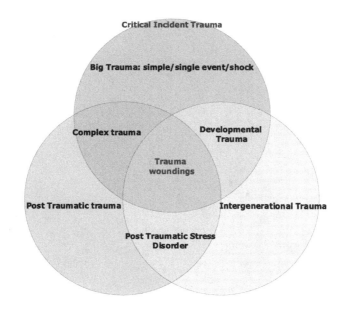

[47] Stephen K., Levine, *Trauma, Tragedy, Therapy. The Arts and Human Suffering* (Jessica Kingsley Publishers, London, 2009), 17.

[48] Cathy A. Malchiodi *Trauma and Expressive Arts Therapy. Brain, Body, & Imagination in the Healing Process*. (The Guildford Press, 2020).

Emotional wounding is at the heart of all traumas. But different instances or events when the trauma has occurred have led to the categorizing of the traumas. Critical incident trauma is often referred to as Big T-Trauma. This type of trauma happens because of a single event like an accident or a natural disaster and is experienced as acute. Complex trauma happens because of invasive incidents such as domestic violence or abuse that happened over a prolonged time. Developmental trauma occurs through forms of abuse, mainly attachment figures in a person's life. Historical trauma such as a war, or genocide that happened to families or communities can result in generational or intergenerational trauma. Posttraumatic trauma results when an acute Big T-trauma has not been resolved and acute distress develops into posttraumatic stress over time.

The following table categorizes the trauma events under the type of traumas as identified by psychologists Briere and Scott, and Cathy Malchiodi.[49]

[49] John N Briere and Catherine Scott, *Principles of Trauma Therapy. A Guide to Symptoms, Evaluation, and Treatment*, 2nd ed. (Los Angeles: Sage Publications, 2013),18 -28. And Cathy A. Malchiodi *Trauma and Expressive Arts Therapy. Brain, Body, & Imagination in the Healing Process.* (The Guildford Press, 2020), 13.

Trauma Categories

TABLE 1

Critical Incident Trauma	Complex Trauma	Developmental Trauma	Post-Traumatic Stress Disorder	Generational, Intergenerational and Historical Trauma
"Actual or threatened death or serious injury, experience or witnessed" or "threat to the physical integrity of self"[50] (DSM-5-TR). It is also called Big T-trauma, simple trauma, single event, or shock trauma; acute trauma. Trauma that occurs in a workplace has personal as well as organizational impacts. [51] Workplace trauma is common among first responders, military personnel (Brooks et al., 2019), and social and health workers (Devilly et al., 2009) who work with children exposed to maltreatment and abuse.	Describes the experience of multiple and/or chronic and prolonged, developmentally adverse traumatic events, most often interpersonal, like sexual or physical abuse, war, community violence, and early-life onset trauma.	A type of trauma that involves significant relationships – our attachment figures, i.e., parents, grandparents, teachers, or caregivers.	Trauma occurs when individuals experience significant symptoms such as feeling out of control, night terrors, difficulty sleeping, flashbacks, avoidance of sounds, light, places, and gaps in memory.[4] It happens when acute trauma has not resolved and has turned into chronic trauma.	It is trauma passed down from those who directly experience it to subsequent generations. The trauma incident may begin with individual trauma or event. However, it can be a collective population in a community (cultural or ethnic) that becomes historical trauma that eventually affects larger populations.

[50] "Individuals with PTSD often report impaired executive functioning, including difficulties with memory and concentration. Influential cognitive models theorize that these difficulties arise when considerable amounts of information processing resources are allocated toward task-irrelevant trauma-related thoughts, feelings, and behaviors at the expense of other emotion-neutral cognitive operations." In C.R. Brewin, & E.A. Holmes (2003). Psychological theories of posttraumatic stress disorder. Clinical Psychology Review, 23(3), 339–376. Accessed January 20.2023, https://doi.org/10.1016/S0272-7358(03)00033-3.

[51] Heponiemi et al., 2014; Strolin-Goltzman et al., 2010 and Brooks et al., 2019, in Morris, H., Hatzikiriakidis, K., Dwyer, J., Lewis, C., Halfpenny, N., Miller, R., & Skouteris, H. Early Intervention for Residential Out-of-Home Care Staff Using Eye Movement Desensitization and Reprocessing (EMDR). Psychological Trauma: Theory, Research, Practice, and Policy, Accessed December 22,2022, https://dx.doi.org/10.1037/tra0001418

Trauma types:	Trauma types:	Trauma types:	Trauma types:	Trauma types:
Natural Disasters, Large-Scale Transportation Accidents, Fire and burns, motor vehicle accidents, sudden death, rape and sexual assault, stranger assault, witnessing or being confronted with homicide or suicide, life-threatening medical conditions, emergency exposure to trauma, war, torture.	Child abuse, mass interpersonal violence, sex trafficking, and intimate partner violence.	Abandonment, in vitro trauma, birth trauma, and childhood trauma. Children and young people with a lived experience of trauma can exhibit aggressive and violent behaviour, emotional dysregulation, and have a poor understanding of social interactions.[52]	Critical incidents, war and all the life-threatening events experienced during traumatic occurrences	The Holocaust, The Ukrainian Holodomor genocide. Residential schools in Canada and Australia. The genocide in Rwanda.

[52] Aebi et al., 2017, Dvir et al., 2014, Richey et al., 2016, in Morris, H., Hatzikiriakidis, K., Dwyer, J., Lewis, C., Halfpenny, N., Miller, R., & Skouteris, H. (2022, December 22). Early Intervention for Residential Out-of-Home Care Staff Using Eye Movement Desensitization and Reprocessing (EMDR). Psychological Trauma: Theory, Research, Practice, and Policy, accessed December 22, 2022, https://dx.doi.org/10.1037/tra0001418

CHAPTER

TRAUMA IN THE BIBLE

Scripture is filled with trauma narratives. Christians identify with traumatic loss when they identify Jesus's unbearable sorrow on the cross. Deborah van Deusen Hunsinger explains, "We behold a crucified Savior, a God who bears our grief and carries our sorrow, who heals by taking away the sin of the world, both the evil we suffer and the evil we do."[53] Through participation in Holy Communion, we identify with Christ in His death and his suffering. However, there is comfort in knowing that when trauma victims discover God's divine love, they will also learn that Jesus was willing to bear what is unbearable for mortal, fallen human beings. Van Deusen states,

> "If God in Jesus Christ descends into the worst hell imaginable in order to deliver us from the hells we inflict upon one another, then such a God is worthy of our trust. We need not stand by helplessly witnessing the suffering and dying of those we love; we have a God to whom we can entrust them in life and death. ... As the creeds of the church attest,
>
> He is known to us as the risen Lord, the very Wisdom, and Power of God, through whom God will fulfill his purpose of redemption. Jesus Christ, the gospel attests,

<hr>

[53] Ibid., 13.

bears what cannot be borne by fragile, fallen human beings. He alone bears the sin of the world, and he alone bears it away."[54]

To see how Scripture framed trauma and emotional distress, let us turn to the Book of Job to explore his encounter with suffering through a trauma-informed lens. Known as "one of the oldest books of the Bible"[55] the book interchanges from a short introduction in prose to expand into beautiful poetry. Introducing Job as its protagonist, theologian Isabelle Hamley explains, "The careful juxtaposition of prose and poetry suggests a man whose faith was anchored in his community's traditional expressions of spirituality. In the face of incomprehensive suffering, his certainties start to crumble...The book becomes a story of trauma and how the community of faith may facilitate or hinder constructive responses to psychological pain."[56] Hamley describes that in the prose prologue, as introduced in Job 1:1-5, we encounter Job during his pre-trauma period when his life was first-rate, able to worship and sacrifice to God. She believes Job had "A traditional tendency to think of suffering as punishment for wrongdoing."[57] During this time Job's life was predictable and orderly. Hamley noted that it seems

---

[54] Deborah Van Deusen Hunsinger, *Bearing the Unbearable. Trauma, Gospel, and Pastoral Care* (Grand Rapids, Michigan: William B Eerdmans Publishers Company, 2015), 13.

[55] "The question of the authorship of the book, is a very complicated one, and there are many views advanced. The view of the date and authorship of the book which seems to be most free from objection regards the book as composed at some time during the reign of Solomon. The view was advanced by Martin Luther, and during the nineteenth century was defended by Haevernick, Keil and Delitzsch. The positive arguments in its favour bear throughout the stamp of that creative, beginning period of the Chokma – of that Solomonic age of knowledge and art, of deeper thought respecting revealed religion, and of intelligent, progressive culture of the traditional forms of art – that unprecedented age in which the literature corresponded to the summit of glorious magnificence to which the kingdom of the promise had then attained. According to one alternate view expressed in *Baba Batra* 14b, Moses was the author of Job. Those who have supported this view have been accustomed to point to the presence in Job of certain words which also occur in the Pentateuch, such as 'ulam, tnu" ah, netz, pelilim, qshitah, yeret." Edward J. Young, *An Introduction to the Old Testament* (Grand Rapids, Michigan: William B Eerdmans Publishing Co. 1978), 319 - 320.

[56] Christopher C.H. Cook and Isabelle Hamley, *The Bible and Mental Health: Towards a Biblical Theology of Mental Health* (London: SCM Press,2020), 85.

[57] Ibid, 86.

as if Job's faith was based on routine practices which he performed almost compulsively. We find him continually sacrificing before God to atone for his children in case they have sinned. The question for me arises whether it is possible that Job at this juncture in his life has not experienced, understood, or integrated the concept of grace into his worship before God yet. Michael V. Fox suggests an alternative to Hamley's stance, arguing that the book "presupposes God's basic concern for justice …and that God does reward the righteous. Job is introduced in verse 1 as "innocent and honest, fearing God and avoiding evil," and verses 2–4 report on his prospering." He finds it impossible to read this sequence as other than causal: Job prospered because he was righteous."[58] Aside from whether Job was materially blessed and emotionally secure because of his works or because of God's grace, from a trauma perspective it is noteworthy that people need some agency to feel safe and operate with confidence. Job's life appeared to reflect emotional stability at the time, a precondition for contentment in solid relationships. Described as a blameless, upright, and God-fearing man, Job was blessed in all facets of his life. However, this stability did not last. Job's story shifted suddenly and radically, through the dramatic impacts of a conversation in the heavenlies. Hamley expands on the exchange that was taking place between God (*Yahweh*) and the 'accuser' (*ha-satan*) as recorded in Job Chapter 1: 6 – 12.[59] When this conversation happens, she notes that there are no lines of communication between Job and the Lord.

I agree that Job's ignorance about Satan is quite evident. When we encounter him for the first time, he is on the verge of disaster and does not know what will happen to him and his family. Job did not know about the heavenly court, nor was he aware of the case surrounding him that was going on in the court of heaven.[60] We read in Job 1:6 – Job 2:6 how Satan, our adversary, was contending for his demise. Satan hates the fact that God delights in His children and their wellbeing. As the court

---

[58] Michael V. Fox; The Meanings of the Book of Job. *Journal of Biblical Literature* 1 April 2018; 137 (1): 9. https://doi.org/10.15699/jbl.1371.2018.1372.

[59] Job 1:6 "Now there was a day when the sons of God came to present themselves before the LORD, and Satan also came among them."

[60] Robert Henderson, *Operating in Courts of Heaven*. (Shippensburg, PA: Destiny Image Publishers, 2021).

case continued, Job's secure and stable lifestyle, filled with rituals and meaning and purpose to him and his loved ones, was cruelly interrupted by repeated traumatic experiences and loss. With his possessions taken, the message of his children's death, and his body in acute physical pain, Job is stripped of everything. Life as he knows it, is falling apart. With this comes a change in how he engages with God. It alters his view on life. Fox observes how Job's dialogue in Chapter 3 shows how his view of God became fractured.[61] Job is experiencing severe trauma symptoms where his personhood is shaken to its core, and he desires to die:

"May the day perish on which I was born... why did I not die at birth? ... Why is light given to him who is in misery... to a man whose way is hidden? For my sighing comes before I eat, and my groanings pour out like water.

For the thing I greatly feared has come upon me, and what I dreaded has happened to me. I am not at ease, nor am I quiet; I have no rest, for trouble comes" (Job 3:1 – 26).

Based on what we know about Stephen Porges's Polyvagal theory, and the principle of neuroception, "Which is the nervous system's evaluation of risk in the environment without conscious awareness,"[62] we know that Job is not isolated in his anguish and pain. His wife and friends suffer with him. They are impacted by his trauma also. Most people who have encountered severe trauma can identify with Job. They, too, cannot see in the heavenly sphere and they do not fully understand the script of God's ultimate story in their lives. For believers who suffer from trauma, it is affirming to know that Job was also overwhelmed. Not knowing how to make meaning of their suffering, those suffering from trauma often feel helpless. Some question their relationship with God, while others turn their back on their faith because they no longer understand Him, or what to believe about His love for humanity. They

---

[61] Michael V. Fox; The Meanings of the Book of Job. *Journal of Biblical Literature* 1 April 2018; 137 (1): 7–18. https://doi.org/10.15699/jbl.1371.2018.1372, 10.

[62] Stephen W. Porges, *The Pocket Guide to the Polyvagal Theory. The Transformative Power of Feeling Safe.* (New York: W.W. Norton & Company, 2017), 143.

might question the Lord's love for them. Hamley expounds on God's character and says the Book of Job demonstrates that "God is not unambiguous – not simply portrayed as a God of love or justice."[63] For people who have suffered from trauma, the awareness that God is omnipresent but not single-dimensionally at work is important.

Suffering is complex. Like Job, people wrestle with their faith, ask difficult questions from God, and seek meaning beyond what seems obvious or religiously acceptable. Job shares in their alienation from self, others, and God. Hamley explains that this biblical narrative "Takes us on a journey with Job and his friends as they grope towards a way of being, individually and collectively, in the face of deep grief and trauma. Job's experiences shake up the foundations of not only his faith but also that of community."[64] Processing the fragmentation caused by loss, self-doubt, grief, and trauma stuck at a cellular level in people's bodies is critical. It invades their memories, their sleep, and their thoughts. Trauma impacts all dimensions of a person's being and existence and aligns with how Van Deusing Hunsinger explains the effects of trauma, to be

> [a] series of nested concentric circles, affecting every level of our lives, beginning with the suffering involved in facing our mortality and personal capacity for evil and reaching progressively outward to trauma with greater scope... Finally, in the outermost circle of hell, we encounter not only the terror of natural and ecological disasters but also the moral catastrophes of war, torture, genocide, and terrorism.[65]

In the context of Job's story, I think the depth of traumatic impact and degree of helplessness is daunting. His experience reflects the cumulative contagion of how individual trauma spills over to affect relationships, family, and community. For Job, this resulted in a

---

[63] Christopher C.H. Cook and Isabelle Hamley, *The Bible and Mental Health: Towards a Biblical Theology of Mental Health* (London: SCM Press, 2020), 87.

[64] Ibid., 85.

[65] Deborah Van Deusen Hunsinger, *Bearing the Unbearable. Trauma, Gospel, and Pastoral Care* (Grand Rapids, Michigan: William B Eerdmans Publishers Company, 2015), xi.

whirlwind of chaos that eventually absorbed everything in his life. Below is a graphic summary of how I visualize Van Deusen Hunsinger's circling effect, when she explains how trauma explodes and expands to implode everything in a person's normal life (see fig.3).

TRAUMA'S IMPACT EXPLODES

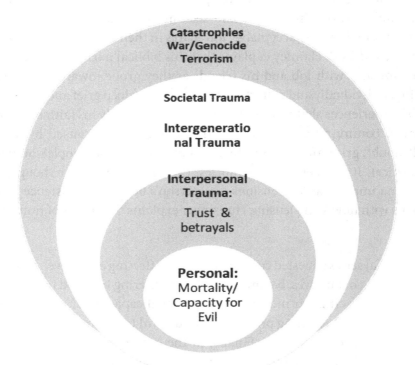

Catastrophies War/Genocide Terrorism

Societal Trauma

Intergeneratio nal Trauma

Interpersonal Trauma:
Trust & betrayals

Personal:
Mortality/ Capacity for Evil

Following Job's story of pain, where his wife and friends are also pulled into the whirlwind of chaos and pain, we see how trauma processing begins to take shape. The good news is that Job's story of trauma does not end in disaster. Although trauma is destructive and reaches far and wide, the Lord's children are not helpless victims in the face of trauma. God remains in control. He is the Alpha and the Omega. Through venting and questioning, Job takes the opportunity to reflect and turn to God, time and again. And then, *out of the whirlwind* God broke through into Job's world, and spoke to him, " And I will ask you, and you instruct Me!" (Job 38:1 -3). Fox said that contrary to what Job feared when God appeared, (Job 9:17-18), he did not terrify Job into submission. Instead, He challenged Job to gird his loins and prepare himself for a conversation. "God's speech is not spoken in anger and arrogance… He used a tone of didactic persuasiveness and painted a picture of a well-tended word…God cares for his creatures."[66] When God reminded Job about Genesis, about the glorious beginning of this earth, he was reminded of the Creator, the Lord in all His might, wisdom and power. Job rediscovered the source and purpose of his existence, and why he does not have to fear. He encountered the Fountain of Life.

Meaning-making is an important part of trauma processing that results in life integration. When Job encounters God's grace it solicits gratitude, and he responds: "I have heard of Thee by the hearing of the ear; But now my eye sees Thee; Therefore, I retract, I repent in dust and ashes." (Job 42:5,6). Yahweh challenges Job and offers him a haven; courageously, Job responds with authenticity and vulnerability. Surrendering to the processing of his humanity he eventually can move on with his life. Job has encountered mercy in the place of judgment and condemnation. This changes how he engages on behalf of others, instead of offering sacrifices on their behalf, he can pray for his friends, allowing them to sacrifice for themselves afterwards.

With Job's story in mind, we see how trauma shakes people's sense of safety and belonging; it infringes on their relationships, shatters their entire personhood; robs them of hope; and affects their bodies. However, Scripture provides us with a hope-filled approach to trauma treatment where Christians can be invited to celebrate even during times of trial and suffering. Christ did not only identify with our sorrow and shame, but He also rose victoriously out of the fire of hell to bear our pain. He is the Risen Lord. When believers, trusting in God, prayerfully and willingly address their trauma, Holy Spirit is faithful to help bring meaning-making and integration. What a comfort, what a hope!

---

[66] Michael V. Fox; The Meanings of the Book of Job. *Journal of Biblical Literature* 1 April 2018; 137 (1): 7–18. https://doi.org/10.15699/jbl.1371.2018.1372, 11 -13.

CHAPTER 3

HOW TO TREAT TRAUMA

Encountering and working with people who suffer from trauma must be addressed with great care. Booking sessions with a pastoral counsellor or trauma-focused therapist is always recommended. Trauma-focused therapists understand trauma theories and can assess for trauma's devastating impact on the person's entire personhood. Staci Haines says that the stressful effects of trauma leave an imprint on the mind, brain, and body, which, according to Van der Kolk, "Has ongoing consequences for how the human organism manages to survive in the present."[67] He says when the thalamus shuts down in the brain to survive the danger, later, after the risk has ceased, the trauma victim does not know which sensory information is relevant and what can safely be ignored. It seems that when trauma is re-triggered afterwards it has an effect deep inside the brain and the organs as well. This must be kept in mind when people are treated for trauma wounds. One thing that most therapists therefore agree on is that talk therapy alone is not enough to address the multilayers of trauma. Haines who advocates for trauma processing to include bodywork says, "Our bodies tell stories. Our muscles hold memories... the "shaping" or "armo[u]ring in a body will not shift unless the concern that causes contraction is taken care of. The person's lack of protection, safety, love, shame or feelings of terror must be worked through. To best resolve trauma, Haines advocates

---

[67] Van Der Kolk, Bessel. *The Body Keeps Score. Brain, Mind, and Body in the Healing of Trauma* (New York, Penguin Books, 2015), 20.

for somatic work to be offered from a neuroscientific perspective. She believes, "The body is the easiest doorway into working with those reactions, emotions, and memories which are primarily run by the reptilian brain, and the limbic and stress centres in the brain...New thinking happens from changes within embodied patterns." [68]

Cathy Malchiodi, a psychologist who treats trauma through expressive arts therapy, resonates with Haines' stance on the importance of trauma treatment that should start in the body. She concludes, "One of the key advantages of the expressive arts in trauma interventions is the ability to circumvent the limits of language and to provide additional channels and opportunities for communication when words are not possible. In this sense, these approaches offer the possibility to externalize implicit experiences without words."[69] Once the trauma event has been isolated and identified, verbal therapies can follow to complete the process in a way that adapts well to cognitive processing. A multimodal approach that includes modalities such as Somatic Experiencing; Neurofeedback; Hypnotherapy; Sensorimotor Psychotherapy; Eye Movement Desensitization; Play therapy; music; art; and expressive arts therapies should be utilized in combination with standard talk therapies to accommodate the full scope of the impacts of trauma on people. Peter Levine who has observed that different people inversely experience the same traumatic event differently, believes that emotional support by people who they trust is a precondition for effective trauma treatment. He says, "traumatized people are unable to overcome the anxiety of their experience, and they are defeated and terrified."[70] He argues for "Deep interconnection, support, and social cohesion as requirements and preconditions for trauma processing to happen."[71] Feeling respected and safe with the person who walks with you when you process your trauma story, is paramount. Choosing the

---

[68] Haines, Staci, K., *The Politics of Trauma: Somatics, Healing and Social Justice.* Berkely: North Atlantic Books, 2019.

[69] Cathy A. Malchiodi *Trauma and Expressive Arts Therapy. Brain, Body, & Imagination in the Healing Process.* (The Guildford Press, 2020), 28.

[70] Peter A. Levine and Ann Frederick, *Waking the Tiger. Healing Trauma. The Innate Capacity to Transform Overwhelming Experiences* (Berkeley, California: North Atlantic Books, 1997), 28.

[71] Ibid., 32.

right person to be your therapist or accountability partner while you engage with the art directive reflections in the book is therefore very important.

MEMORY REPROCESSING

Trauma alters our memories and how these memories have been stored in the brain. Van Der Kolk explains that traumatic memories are disorganized and "Fundamentally different from the stories we tell about the past. They are dissociated: "The different sensations that entered the brain during the trauma are not properly assembled into a story, a piece of autobiography."[72] Fragmented memories leave people stuck, continually impacted by the past while in the present. Creative art interventions and reflections about trauma assist and the process produce a more integrated experience, more manageable and meaningful memories, and a clearer understanding of the experience—in both existential terms, and with a concrete beginning, middle, and end to the memory itself. When that happens, the reconstructed memory allows the person to become more adaptable to the present. Once integration of the memory as a complete while has occurred, access to the self is restored, and re-engagement with life can commence.

Levine, who explored the somatic effects of trauma in humans and animals, explains that the genetic memory of the traumatic event could persist in the brain and nervous system for years after the event. He says, "Because the physiological mechanism that governs the primitive, instinctual parts of our brains and nervous system is not under our conscious control, the immobility response happens involuntarily."[73] He advocates for people to learn how to recognize these initial responses to danger that persists in the body. Levine describes it as a felt sense, which manifests with four components that are always recognizable:

---

[72] Van Der Kolk, Bessel. *The Body Keeps Score. Brain, Mind, and Body in the Healing of Trauma* (New York, Penguin Books, 2015), 196.
[73] Levine, Peter A, and Ann Frederick. *Waking the Tiger. Healing Trauma. The Innate Capacity to Transform Overwhelming Experiences* (Berkeley, California: North Atlantic Books, 1997), 17.

hyperarousal; constriction; dissociation; [and] freezing (immobility) associated with the feeling of helplessness. [74] He argues that if these "Immense energies that have originally created the symptoms of trauma could be properly engaged and mobilized, [it] can transform the trauma and propel us into new heights of healing, mastery, and even wisdom. Trauma resolved is a great gift, returning us to the natural world of ebb and flow, harmony, love, and compassion."[75] If we embrace the traumatic events in our lives as an opportunity to learn new life lessons we can learn from and grow, our lives become richer and filled with more opportunities for gratitude.

THE DIFFERENT PHASES OF TRAUMA TREATMENT

What are the conditions for a trauma treatment plan to be effective in supporting a person's full life integration? Internationally accepted practice guidelines for trauma treatment hold to a three-phase progression for trauma processing to happen effectively. Armstrong introduces the three phases of trauma-informed therapy, as "Phase I: Create Safety, Hope and Therapeutic Alliance...Phase II: Transform Traumatic Memories...Phase III: Facilitate Post-Traumatic Growth." [76] I used the treatment guidelines and principles established by the respected and well-known Blue Knot Foundation, Australia's National Centre of Excellence for Complex Trauma Treatment, to develop the directives that were used in this book.[77] Below is a summary of its well-researched treatment phases.

---

[74] Ibid., 132.

[75] Ibid., 21.

[76] Courtney Armstrong, *Rethinking Trauma Treatment: Attachment, Memory Reconsolidation and Resilience*. (New York: W.W. Norton & Company, 2019), xii-xiii.

[77] Kezelman, Cathy and Stavropoulos, Pam. *Practice Guidelines for Treatment of Complex Trauma and Trauma Informed Care and Service Delivery*. The Australian Government Department for Health and Aging. Blue Knot Foundation, 2017. Blue Knot Foundation, accessed on December 12, 2022, https://blueknot.org.au/.

PHASE ONE: THERAPEUTIC ALLIANCE, SAFETY, ASSESSMENT AND STABILIZATION

A person who experiences an acutely dysregulated emotional state because of a crisis needs stabilization and regulation. Establishing emotional rapport and maintaining a feeling of emotional safety throughout the time that you address your trauma is vital. Feeling a sense of belonging and acceptance from someone makes it easier to feel secure and safe. Having a healthy bond with a therapist or your accountability partner helps to address ruptured relationships and attachments which could have been caused by or were indirectly because of the trauma. Solid grounding and containment activities help to dissolve accumulated and pent-up stress, which is stored in your body, and can manifest as "chronic bodily reactions because of the trauma." As described in the DSMI-5-TR.[78]

Peter Levine believes the key to healing traumatic symptoms lies in being able to mirror the fluid adaptations of animals to take out and pass through the immobility response of trauma "to become fully mobile and functional again."[79] During phase one work, people can engage with bodywork to 'shake' the immobility out of the body. Further to this is the concept of therapeutic stabilization. People must feel safe enough to think and engage with their feelings simultaneously. For them to make informed, practical, and logical choices, they must be

---

[78] American Psychiatric Association, *Diagnostic Statistical Manual of Mental Disorders Fifth Edition Text Revision,* DSM-5-TR. Washington: American Psychiatric Association Publishing, Washington, DC. 2022. 303, 218.

[79] "Traumatic symptoms are not caused by the "triggering" event itself. They stem from the frozen residue of energy that has not been resolved and discharged; this residue remains trapped in the nervous system where it can wreak havoc on our bodies and spirits. The long-term alarming, debilitating, and often bizarre symptoms of PTSD develop when we cannot complete the process of moving in, through and out of the "immobility" or "freezing" state. However, we can thaw by initiating and encouraging our innate drive to return to a state of dynamic equilibrium. ... The difference between the inner racing of the nervous system (engine) and the body's outer immobility (brake) creates a forceful turbulence inside the body similar to a tornado. The tornado of energy is the focal point of which form the symptoms of traumatic stress." In Levine, Peter A, and Ann Frederick. *Waking the Tiger. Healing Trauma. The Innate Capacity to Transform Overwhelming Experiences* (Berkeley, California: North Atlantic Books, 1997),19,20.

able to engage with concepts holistically. Apart from having a solid relationship with someone, one also needs to be aware of the risk factors that were triggered because of trauma. This means that you must engage in a thorough assessment of the risk factors like potential self-harm, suicidal thoughts or other symptoms of trauma before you start with trauma processing. If your trauma is such that you contemplate hurting yourself or someone else, do not delay and reach out to a professional as soon as possible. If you feel confident that you can harness and protect yourself, the last chapters of this book will be helpful to you. You will learn and read about self-regulation, breathing, grounding, and self-awareness integration skills. One of the very painful responses to trauma is often intense feelings of shame or guilt. According to Paul Frewen and Ruth Lanius, "In many traumatized persons, the experience of shame essentially *defines who they are* ... [the person will move] from fear or anxiety to the sense of a *'damaged self.'"*[80] Living with guilt and shame is deeply painful and can prevent people from living lives that feel meaningful. Addressing shame effectively is paramount for emotional growth and personal self-worth. This is why reading and working through the last chapters of the book will be helpful to you.

PHASE TWO: TRAUMA PROCESSING AND TRAUMA MEMORY RECONSOLIDATION

Processing the trauma becomes possible once you have learned to self-regulate your emotions. Self-regulation and dual awareness are critical pre-conditions for effective trauma processing. We know that the traumatized person must first experience safety and how to contain their feelings, even though they potentially could be triggered to experience emotional flooding and discomfort during the reparative interventions again. We call this ability to acknowledge your feelings and contain the emotions around it, the process of dual awareness. Janina Fisher explains that when a person uses dual awareness, they can "Fully inhabit the moment: to feel [their] feet on the ground through awareness of body

---

[80] Paul Frewen and Ruth Lanius, *Healing the Traumatized Self* (New York: Norton, 2015), 206.

sensation while [their]visual perception takes in details of the room in which [they]are sitting – while, in the same moment, [they] can evoke an image from an earlier time in [their] lives that takes [them] 'back there' to a state-specific memory."[81] So, for the re-processing of traumatic memories, a person must be able to tolerate the different sensations linked to the critical incident that caused the trauma in the first place.

For trauma treatment to be effective, one must acknowledge the uniqueness of each person and the fact that each one of them will therefore process their trauma in their preferred way. About this uniqueness in the minds of people, Van Der Kolk observes,

> "[T]he mind is a mosaic and [w]e all have parts...the parts form a network or system in which change in any one part will affect all the others... these extreme parts bear the burden of the trauma...Each split-off part holds different memories, beliefs, and physical sensations; some hold the shame, others the rage, some the pleasure and excitement, another the intense loneliness of the abject compliance...The critical insight is that all these parts have a function: to protect the self from feeling the full terror of annihilation." [82]

In alignment with Darryl Stephen's view, who sees psychological trauma as a protective response, each of these affected 'parts' of the person's system can be understood as functioning to protect the person during a crisis. These parts must be identified, named, and accordingly processed. Blue Knot's guidelines stress that trauma phase two work should encompass and attune to all the visible and non-verbal indicators of the person's expression, behaviour, movement, and the fluctuating dynamic of hyperarousal and hypo-arousal as explored in the Polyvagal theory. Though it might be difficult, all therapeutic interventions must be such that the person can leave after they have worked on their trauma and still feel as if they are in control, and with an embodied adult state.

---

[81] Janina Fisher, *Healing the Fragmented Selves of Trauma Survivors* (New York: Routledge, 2017), 78.

[82] Bessel Van Der Kolk, *The Body Keeps Score. Brain, Mind, and Body in the Healing of Trauma* (New York: Penguin Books, 2015), 282 - 284.

When you engage in therapy or participate by doing the therapeutic directives, always try to remain aware of the present. Tell yourself *where* you are, *what time it is* and *who* you are. The specific strategies and tools you will be introduced to in the book will help to regulate your emotions in the face of any potential activation you could experience when you are not engaged with trauma processing.

PHASE THREE: INTEGRATION AND MAINTENANCE

During the third phase's execution, post-traumatic growth and re-engagement with life are taking place. During this phase, the focus is on implementing the skills you have acquired during the trauma processing, in your day-to-day functioning, and when you interact in relationships. Research by Lawrence Calhoun and Richard Tedeschi has identified five different areas where people have reported health in their lives after trauma encounters: By accepting their own vulnerabilities, people became more courageous and had a greater sense of personal strength in their lives; they opened themselves up to new possibilities; experienced a greater appreciation for life; encountered growth in their spirituality; and, finally, they benefited from improved relationships.[83] Kosha Joubert says, "When we take responsibility for our past, we [are enabled]… to take responsibility for our future. When we dare to go to the roots of the crisis, together, to acknowledge and learn from what happened, we prepare the seeds for post-traumatic growth."[84] If trauma has been processed well, the person will find that they are hopeful and want to engage with life again. As you continue working on and processing your trauma, it is a good idea to begin seeking out some meaningful engagements and healthy relationships again, if you have lost some. People who have processed their trauma stories effectively are hopeful about the future and will not be afraid to engage in the world around them. For Christians, it implies they will want to reconnect

---

[83] L.G. Calhoun & R.G. Tedeschi, *Facilitating Posttraumatic Growth: A Clinician's Guide* (Kindle Edition). (New York: Taylor and Francis, 2008).
[84] Kosha Joubert, C+ Pocket Project, https://pocketproject.org.

meaningfully with their church community and engage with passion in their relationship with God. Thomas Huebl, the founder of the Pocket Project, a global restoration movement, and working with an organization dedicated to growing a culture of trauma-informed care says, "Every time trauma is healed, we restore a part of our past and make possible a brighter future for ourselves and succeeding generations. We transform separation, othering, and scarcity into relation, interdependence, and abundance."[85]

For the community of believers who align themselves with efforts to help trauma victims, the principles of restorative practices must also be in motion to help these people who have suffered trauma. Debora van Deusen Hunsinger explains restorative practices as "A way to promote mutual understanding, self-responsibility, and effective action in communities torn apart by conflict or shocked by trauma...[B]ecause forgiveness and reconciliation lie at the core of the gospel, the church, for the sake of its basic integrity, needs to be tireless in aligning its relational practices with its beliefs."[86]

In conclusion, trauma results after a deeply painful or alarming experience that has overwhelmed a person's psyche, leaving an emotional injury. Like an untouched physical wound, if not treated, the aftereffects of the psychological wounding can lead to long-lasting ruptures to safety and wellbeing. The impact of the injury is multidimensional and does not only affect the individual on a psychosocial and spiritual level. Trauma is also stored in the body. Because their entire personhood is affected by the fact that they no longer feel safe, how a person views the world and engages in relationships with others and the Lord, is also impacted. Trauma does not only invade the person's immediate world but also how they perceive their past. It robs people of hope and consequently, they do not engage with the future. The initial critical event and trauma associated with the event have a rippling effect even further impacting communities and generations to come.

By God's design, people are resilient. This is good news. Job's story from the Bible and what we now know about neuroscience, and how

---

[85] Thomas Huebl, https://pocketproject.org.

[86] Deborah Van Deusen Hunsinger, *Bearing the Unbearable. Trauma, Gospel, and Pastoral Care.* (Grand Rapids, Michigan: William B Eerdmans Publishers Company, 2015),146.

God has designed the brain to restore itself, confirms that even during traumatic times, the Lord cares, and remains involved in people's lives. The concept of neuroplasticity has shown us how trauma injury, when treated well, can assist people in adapting to life, even after trauma. Assisting with effective trauma treatment requires a purposeful plan that serves to process the complex layers of the emotional and mental fragmentation caused by the trauma. Because trauma is stored in the body, addressing it somatically must also be included in the treatment plan.

Internationally accepted trauma treatments are holistic in their approach and incorporate three stages or phases. The first phase's goal is to create emotional safety for the person and allow for the ability to engage safely with the self. It is aimed to address the trauma where it started, which is at the time when people have been vulnerable and stripped of their security and sense of self, without the choice or ability to change the situation or the outcomes of the event. Trauma therefore leaves people in a perpetual state of incompletion. Memories of the event are fragmented and introduce themselves unsolicited at any given time. The second phase assists in transforming these traumatic memories to establish new thought patterns and reconstructed memories. This phase takes time and must be done carefully to ensure people are not retraumatized. The third phase of trauma treatment facilitates posttraumatic growth where the person experiences hope-infused, creative, and healthy re-integration with life. At this stage, people are encouraged to participate in collective practices. This can include active service in the community and their congregations. Other Church members can play a positive role in this recovery. We know that even though trauma affects humanity at the core of its existence if addressed and processed well, it results in people discovering their own inner strength and resolve. This helps them to discover new and creative ways to engage with the world. Because their spirit became alive, and their relationship with God has been strengthened due to what they have endured, their personal and intimate relationships have been enhanced after the trauma has been resolved. Yes, trauma, when processed well, can and should be celebrated.

CHAPTER 4

THE UNDERPINNINGS FOR
A TRAUMA TREATMENT
THAT CONSIDERS
BIBLICAL PRINCIPLES

Traumatized people inhabit the story of their psychological injury from which they feel and believe they are unable to escape. The previous chapter highlights that painful flashback images occur due to fragmented trauma memories which are stored in different areas of the brain and the body to involuntarily re-introduce themselves whenever experiences or sensations related to the trauma are triggered. Because the trauma story has not concluded, the psychological pain endures. The trauma victim has developed a new narrative defined by invasive trauma memories. In addition to this, like what happened to Job, believers who have experienced trauma find that the effects of the critical incident, at least in the aftermath of it, hurt their relationship with the Lord as well. If emotional wounding remains unresolved these intrusions can over time, cause systematic fragmentation in their personhood and self-identity, leaving the believer feeling lost, disconnected, and not familiar with their self.

Thus, understanding some facts about identity formation is necessary when you as a believer want to address and curb the potential fragmentation of your personhood and self-identity. In this chapter, I will review the role of narrative and story in identity configuration.

Acknowledging God as the Creator, I will revisit identity formation from a narrative and phenomenological perspective. Because I am convinced that the successful integration of a trauma story into a person's life is only possible with the help of Holy Spirit, I will discuss the Holy Spirit's role during therapeutic artmaking reflections. To be ethically accountable as to how I developed the therapeutic artmaking directives and reflective invitations, I will discuss the guiding principles that informed the normative decisions I made while developing these directives which will be introduced in the last part of the book.

STORY AND NARRATIVE AS PART OF HUMAN EXISTENCE.

Empirical research reveals that theology and psychology have embraced the importance of narrative in their disciplines. This reflects our distinctive human tendency to share life with others through narratives and stories. Paul Ricoeur offers, "We equate life with the story or stories that we can tell about it."[87] People create stories to make sense of their existence and how they encounter the world. Esther Reed explains, "Storytelling is part of the process of meaning-making, of creating order out of chaos and of exploring and articulating our own intuitive knowledge. Across traditions, stories, myths and images dominate as methods of both expressing personal felt-reality and encompassing shared cultural values and ideals."[88] Historically these constructed stories were then repeated over time, also in story format. Stephen Crites argues that "The formal quality of experience through time is inherently narrative." This implies that humans' lived experiences over time can only be expressed through narratives because of time. He concludes "Narrative is fundamentally part of human existence and the human experience."[89]

---

[87] Paul Ricoeur in David Wood *On Paul Ricoeur: Narrative and Interpretation.* (London: Routledge, 1991),191.

[88] Esther D. Reed, Rob Freathy, Susanna Cornwall and Anna Davis. "Narrative Theology in Religious Education." *British Journal of Religious Education*, 2013 Vol. 35, No. 3, 298, https://dx.doi.org/10.1080/01416200.2013.785931.

[89] Stephen Crites in Stanley Hauerwas and Gregory L. Jones, Eds. *Why Narrative? Readings In Narrative Theology.* (Eugene. Oregon: Wipf and Stock Publishers, 1997),66.

In the context of how we use narrative in trauma treatment to address self-identity formation, we must not confuse narrative with narrating. So what is narrating? "Narrating is representing, a re-presenting of events... which are not sensually perceivable to the listener. All poetry, all art, 'makes present' ... [and], embodies."[90] Narrating has to do with a re-telling. Mark Curry explains that,

> Narrating constitutes less a phenomenon of retrospection, but rather and primarily one of prospection and projection. Its unique function lies not in the objectification of memory and in the backward-oriented re-presentation of the past that enables the positioning and self-affirmation of ourselves within a biographic and historic continuum. Rather, what counts is the peculiar dialectic of an anticipated retrospection upon the present.[91]

Using narrative in trauma processing is different. It is not only about the present but more so, about the past as well. We engage with the story with the purpose of retrospection and reflection. When people rehearse a story about an event or experience from the past, they gain new perspectives, enabling them to see how they were situated when the event occurred. For this reason, storytelling is helpful when we want to process our own trauma. Having a story to tell about the event can situate the person away from the trauma, providing the opportunity to review the event as an observer and no longer as a participant. On the other hand, listening to a story as a template in the present, can allow for an opportunity to mirror and reflect on your own trauma story in light of the narrated story. In this instance a narrative about the past is employed for the sake of the now and for the future.

In the context of story, the writer Edward Forster explains that narration is a privileged genre for identity construction, particularly

[90] Jan Christoph Meister, and Wilhelm Schernus. *Time: From Concept to Narrative Construct: A Reader*. Narratologia. Berlin: De Gruyter, 2011), 67. Accessed in June 2023. https://search-ebscohost-com.prov.idm.oclc.org/login.aspx?direct=true&db=nlebk&AN=390868&site=ehost-live.
[91] Mark Currie *About Time. Narrative, Fiction and the Philosophy of Time*. (Edinburgh: Edinburgh UP, 2007),151.

because it requires us to situate ourselves as characters in space and time. "A narrative consists of both a "story" and a "plot". Whereas a story merely presents a chain of events, the plot presents stories that are not only chronologically related but also related in terms of cause and effect."[92] Alister McGrath explains another slight difference between narrative and story and says, "*Narrative* tends to mean that a speaker is reporting what they experienced in a relatively unprocessed way. While *story* tends to imply that the teller has composed a narration that involves a beginning, middle, and end, with meaning added; ... and the option of including Direct Speech by story characters. ... Narratives also involve shaping and assigning meaning to a series of events." [93] When people construct narrations of traumatic events in their lives, they distance themselves from the event and this helps to get a holistic perspective on how the incident occurred and what could have been the cause of the event. This assists in meaning-making to happen.

Living in a storied context is explained by Stephen Crites who states that people live in their stories. He argues these accounts "form sacred stories...because men's sense of self and world is created through them... For these are stories that orient the life of people through time, their lifetime, their individual and corporate experience and their sense of

---

[92] Edward M. Forster, *Aspects of the Novel,* (London and New York: Penguin. 1962), 92.

[93] "Regardless of whether a story character may be an animal, a human, or other -- all stories are about situations. Story listeners can project themselves into and imagine themselves in these situations. They may empathize and identify with and even imitate the characters. Listeners get to practice for living by considering if they might behave similarly to or different from the ways story characters are behaving. Stories can help to give people senses of identity and direction. Self, community, and society are all conceived of and experienced largely in terms of story. Stories are manageable ways to package data and give it meaning, with relatively easy storage in and retrieval from memory. One's story becomes a form of identity, in which the things one chooses to include in the story, and the way one tells the story, can both reflect and shape who one is. Typical guidelines for performance storytelling are: 1) Visualise. 2) Describe. 3) At times, mime story objects. 4) At times, become characters. Every story has an external shell and an emotional center. The external aspect has to do with the story's place and time, and other details. The internal aspect has to do with the relationships, and the yearnings and other emotions, of the characters. It is the internal aspect of stories that readers and listeners connect with on emotional levels." Alister McGrath in Eric Miller "Story and Storytelling in Storytelling Therapy and Expressive Arts Therapy." *Conference Proceedings.* International Expressive Arts Therapy Conference, Chennai (February 2017), 2.

style, to the great powers that establish the reality of their world."[94] People employ narratives and images about their experiences and relationships to understand and interpret who they are and how they relate to others in relationships, family, the community they find themselves in, their society, and the inhabitable world. It will also include how they relate to the Lord.

Paul Ricoeur believes only humans can create stories over time. He says when this happens, a person begins to form a narrative identity, resulting in how they feel about themselves and others, and how they consequently think and behave. Ricoeur brings story as fiction and narrative together and forms the hypothesis that,

> "The constitution of narrative identity, whether it be that of an individual person or of a historical community, was the sought-after site of the fusion between narrative and fiction. We have an intuitive pre-comprehension of this state of affairs: do not human lives become more readily intelligible when they are interpreted in the light of the stories that people tell about them?"[95]

It seems that when people compare life with the stories they can tell about themselves, and the stories that others tell about them as having occurred over time, they are provided with a narrative identity. This is a privilege only afforded to humans, and Ricoeur says,

> These 'life stories' themselves become more intelligible when what one applies to them are the narrative models—plots—borrowed from history or fiction... The epistemological status of autobiography seems to confirm this intuition. It is thus plausible to endorse the following chain of assertions: self-knowledge is an

[94] Stephen Crites in Stanley Hauerwas and L. Gregory Jones. Eds. *Why Narrative? Readings In Narrative Theology.* (Eugene. Oregon: Wipf and Stock Publishers, 1997),70.
[95] Paul Ricoeur in David Wood on Paul Ricoeur: Narrative and Interpretation.(London: Routledge, 1991),188. Accessed 21 July 2023 https://search-ebscohost-com.prov.idm.oclc.org/login.aspx?direct=true&db=nlebk&AN=80129&site=ehost-live.

interpretation; self interpretation, in its turn, finds in narrative, among other signs and symbols, a privileged mediation.[96]

To understand self-identity better, he makes a clear distinction between identity as sameness and identity as selfhood. Ricoeur explains that selfhood can be determined by asking the question 'who did this or that?" "By this, we certify that the action is the property of whoever committed it, that it is his [hers], that it belongs to him [her] personally." According to him, selfhood has to do with our existence and being that can be attributed to concepts such as "being-in-the-world, care, [or] being-with."[97] He expounds on this and says that self-knowledge is self-interpreted and develops over time because of everyday life's natural ebb and flow. For me, this correlates with how, when trauma occurs, each person interprets the traumatic experience as it relates to their personal circumstances and what they experienced when it happened. Trauma is therefore personal, and the story people tell about it is subjective.

To summarize, a narrative is a purely human experience that develops over time. The integration of these narratives about life experiences eventually forms a story about the self, which is stored as memories. Over time, when revisited and recalled, these memories inform new stories as they are experienced and re-narrated. Subsequently, these narrations result in the development and integration or weaving of personhood, ensuing a self-identity that tells people who they are and how they engage with the world they inhabit. So, apart from providing information, stories advise the construction of self-identity and assist in self-discovery. As more stories or experiences are added to the memories, self-identity can change and be adapted over time.

---

[96] Paul Ricoeur in David Wood on Paul Ricoeur: Narrative and Interpretation.(London: Routledge, 1991),188. Accessed 21 July 2023 https://search-ebscohost-com.prov.idm.oclc.org/login.aspx?direct=true&db=nlebk&AN=80129&site=ehost-live.
[97] Ibid.,189 – 198.

USING NARRATIVE FOR THERAPEUTIC INTEGRATION

If internal narratives are a formative lens through which self and meaning-making are constructed, can historical narratives, specifically Scriptural accounts, inform therapeutic trauma treatment? If so, what foundational principles should be applied when a story is taken directly from the Bible and told in tandem with trauma processing? Embedded in my belief that Holy Spirit inspired the Bible, some relevant and contextualized Scriptural accounts can provide us with principles that can drive therapeutic trauma treatment. This belief then carries the potential to become morally formative and life-altering. People live in stories and communicate through them. So did Jesus. Storytelling is also a well-known and acceptable therapeutic tool for Expressive Art Therapies. Furthermore, storytelling is also part of the Christian community's heritage. Alister McGrath argues, "God has shaped the human mind and imagination to be receptive to stories, and ... these stories are echoes or fragments of the Christian 'grand story.' "[98] When people connect to the narratives from the Bible, it provides, according to McGrath, "a comprehensive and integrated framework of meaning that helps individuals transcend their concerns of experience and connect with something greater. "[99]

In this book, two stories are introduced, one the story of Job's trauma and the other the Creation story. Both stories are intensely personal; one embodied, the other relating to faith. Using Scripture during therapeutic interventions is linked to conviction. Michael Goldberg believes, "Religious convictions, which are at the heart of theological reflection, depend on narrative for their intelligibility and significance."[100] How the creation story is communicated to a person who has suffered trauma, matters. Respect is therefore an important factor in how we proceed to let people tell their stories. The reader

---

[98] McGrath, Alister E. *Narrative Apologetics: Sharing the Relevance, Joy, and Wonder of the Christian Faith* (Grand Rapids: Baker Books, 2019), 10.
[99] Ibid., 58.
[100] Michael Goldberg, *Theology and Narrative. A Critical Introduction* (Wipf and Stock, 2001), 12.

engaging with the reflective art-making to process their trauma must feel respected. This is regardless of whether he or she is a believer or not. Even though fallible humans penned it's stories down, the Bible was inspired by Holy Spirit. This correlates with how believers as a community should share the meta-story of God. - It must always be done with reverence. About the narratives of the story of creation and Job's trauma story; Combined these two stories form a collective thread, serving as the compass towards the fountain of Life that people share in community with each other, and our communal relationship with the Triune God.

As I said before, I often use storytelling as a therapeutic intervention. For therapeutic efficiency and relevancy, stories used during interventions must be easy to understand, yet multidimensional and relatable to humanity. Caution must be taken when stories are told about Scripture. It must be shared in context, and other people's beliefs or religions, particularly when a person does not share those beliefs must always be a consideration. With trauma being processed while the person is applying principles derived from the story of creation as a mirror, I approach the narrative as temporal and causal (see footnote[101]). I do so because, during art-making reflections, the story of creation becomes relevant to their personal life story. All of the directives that people are invited to participate in while reading this book, are designed with the conviction that God's Word and his creative power, when manifested through speaking the universe into existence, carries such significant power that has an eternal impact on humanity. Humans exist because God created the world and all it holds. "And God said ...And God made...So God created..." (Gen 1:1-27).

---

[101] "Currently, four basic approaches to the definition of narrative are in use; we may designate these as temporal, causal, minimal, and transactional. The first posits the representation of events in a time sequence as the defining feature of narrative; the second insists that some causal connection, however oblique, between the events is essential; the third and most capacious, ... any statement of an action or event is ipso facto a narrative, since it implies a transformation or transition from an earlier to a later state; the fourth posits that narrative is simply a way of reading a text, rather than a feature or essence found in a text." In Brian Richardson, "Recent Concepts of Narrative and the Narratives of Narrative Theory." Vol.34., No.2. (Summer 2000), 169.

For believers engaging with therapeutic art-making, the story of Christianity is an additional narrative. When they reflect and make art about this story, they mirror and expose Christ's redemptive work. McGrath says, "Christianity tells a story about God, humanity, and the world that pivots around the life, death, and resurrection of Christ. The incarnation gives coherence and focus to the entire Christian narrative and allows us to grasp its relevance for human life and thought. Above all, it expands our vision of reality, helping us realize that we too often satisfy ourselves with inadequate accounts of ourselves in the universe.[102]

In the book, the story of Creation is contextualized. By keeping the story in its context and as close as possible to the original text, Holy Spirit can be trusted to use the unfolding narratives as signposts for people to process their own life stories and mental health processes during the Lectio Divina meditations and the therapeutic phenomenological artmaking interventions that follow.

---

[102] Alister E. McGrath, *Narrative Apologetics: Sharing the Relevance, Joy, and Wonder of the Christian Faith* (Grand Rapids: Baker Books, 2019), 5.

MEMORIES AND SELF-IDENTITY

"Memories are assembled, stored, and storied in the brain."[103] Marianne Leuzinger-Bohleber's research about embodied memories, trauma, and depression connects the body and the mind and states that the memory, "Must first be recorded in images and language."[104] These memories serve to inform people about their identity and personhood, who they are and how they engage with the world and the people around them. When memories can no longer provide an orderly picture of the past, engagement with life feels unstable and can become capricious, resulting in trauma. When memories

---

[103] Memory is a function of the entire organism, the product of complex, dynamic, re-categorising and interactive processes, which are invariably "embodied". "Embodied" not only means "non-verbal": Memory arises by way of a "coupling" of reciprocally influential sensoric and motoric processes. This "coupling" is biologically implemented through neuronal maps embedded in the organism's sensomotoric system… "[K]nowledge storing" in the dynamic models of embodied cognitive science, though less exact, precisely through this quality, enables optimum generalisation and adaption to a new situation. In the process, so-called neuronal maps are produced through the functional circulation of the organism's constant interaction with its environment. These consist of several 10,000s of neurons, which work functionally in one direction. Thus, each system of perception has, e.g. the visual apparatus, the sensuous surface of the skin etc, and a multiplicity of maps which are stimulated by qualitatively different impressions: colour, touch, direction, warmth etc. These maps are connected to one another by parallel and reciprocal fibres, which guarantee the renewed and repeated entry, flow and exchange of signals. If one map is selected by way of the stimulation of groups of neurons, then a stimulation of the maps to which it is connected simultaneously results. Due to the reciprocal connections ("re-entry"), the nerve impulses are returned, whereby the reinforcement or attenuation of synapsis in the neuronal groups occurs in the synapses of each map: the connections of the maps themselves undergo modification. Through this, new selective qualities emerge, in other words, "automatic" re-categorizations of current stimuli from different sense channels…Through such "sensomotoric coordination", which is connected with permanent re-categorisations, the organism ensures a sustained ability to orient itself in the environment, namely, to connect current experience with previous experience whereby, due to the new situation, previous re-categorisations are adapted by way of the retained stimuli. In Marianne Leuzinger-Bohleber. *Finding the Body in the Mind: Embodied Memories, Trauma, and Depression*. The International Psychoanalytical Association Psychoanalytic Ideas and Applications Series. (London, United Kingdom: Routledge, 2015), 26 - 27. https://search-ebscohost-com.prov.idm.oclc.org/login.aspx?direct=true&db=nlebk&AN=1016526&site=ehost-live.

[104] Ibid., 24.

become scattered, the person is physically, emotionally, mentally, and spiritually affected. Over time, the fragmentation destabilizes selfhood where life, as the person came to know it, is no longer clear and coherent. Jocelyn Bryan says that,

> The role of narrative in personal identity and meaning-making is significant for mental health. The events of our lives, our interpretation of them, and what we feel about them are stored in narrative form in memory. But the interpretation of the story of our past is [also] shaped by what we hope for and imagine in the future. [105]

Memories not only inform people about their history, their present surroundings, and the people they encounter, but also who they are in the world they inhabit. Additionally, thinking and seeing themselves within the context of humanity, they draw from these memories to engage with others, and with the future. Tamara Townsend states, "Memories help to shape a person's personhood and self-identity." To make sense of themselves, people recall memories and stories from their past. In addition, she says that people need to remember, "In order to understand and evaluate the effect of the past on the present ... it serves ... to resolve the dissonance in ... self-understanding."[106] Believers draw from their memories to know what their relationship with the Lord feels like, what they believe about Him, and how they should engage with God. Indeed, memories inform the entire life story. Throughout the Old Testament, we read that God used memory through recalling stories to help the Israelites recall his faithfulness and fidelity.

Townsend explains, "Memory can be described quantitatively by neuroscience and by cognitive psychology, in the working of the brain or the behaviour of the remembering subject, or theoretically in terms of memory's impact on epistemology and ontology and it makes an impact on nearly all human functions, but it can also be seen as mysterious

---

[105] Jocelyn Bryan, *Human Being: Insights from Psychology and the Christian Faith.* (London: SCM Press, 2016), 51.
[106] Ibid.,10.

and unpredictable as life itself."[107] Noteworthy is that our memories do not faithfully reproduce past scenes. Townsend suggests, "Memory does not simply entail storing and recalling, but rather interpreting, shaping, and even inventing details so that the re-created story from the past coheres with the present."[108] Sue Campbell elaborates, "Scientists now explain we combine information from various times in our past with information from the present, and with general knowledge, our imaginings, and the views of others to creatively reconstruct a rendering of our past experiences."[109] All of these imaginings accumulate and over time serve as building blocks towards stability until, according to Townsend, "A narrative of memory establishes a person's identity as relatively stable and unified across time, even while life circumstances keep changing."[110]

Trauma treatment should therefore assist with memory integration that helps people to re-establish a stable self-identity, authentically engage with life, and take responsibility for their choices. The goal is to aid people in reprocessing their memories so that meaning-making and self-integration can happen to such an extent that the event itself—not the chronological sequence of events—and why it happened, can make sense as a coherent whole. Noteworthy, research indicates this self-authenticating integration is both psychological and biological. When memories follow each other chronologically over time, it contributes to logical processing and helps the person to come to conclusions. Trauma events have hijacked these memories and caused fragmented memory recollection. Afterwards this causes difficulty in the recollection

[107] Tamara L. Townsend. *Memory and Identity in the Narratives of Soledad Puértolas : Constructing the Past and the Self.* (Lanham, Maryland: Lexington Books, 2014),11. https://search-ebscohost-com.prov.idm.oclc.org/login.aspx?direct=true&db=nlebk&AN=846022&site=ehost-live.

[108] Ibid., 12.

[109] Sue Campbell, *Relational Remembering*, 4 -5; In Jens Brockmeier "From the End to the Beginning: Retrospective Teleology in Autobiography," in *Narrative and Identity: Studies in Autobiography, Self and Culture*, ed. Jens Brockmeier and Donald Carbaugh. Amsterdam: Benjamins, 2001, 251 – 53.

[110] Tamara L. Townsend. *Memory and Identity in the Narratives of Soledad Puértolas : Constructing the Past and the Self.*(Lanham, Maryland: Lexington Books, 2014),12. https://search-ebscohost-com.prov.idm.oclc.org/login.aspx?direct=true&db=nlebk&AN=846022&site=ehost-live.

of thoughts. When the trauma story has been effectively addressed through an intervention, it forms a new narrative. This means the gap in the trauma-infected thought loop has been closed. Now the recollection of the memory can be concluded. This memory integrates into a new narrative. The recall of the event and how it transpires becomes cohesive as a new sequence in the brain. Bruce Wexler explains, "Recovery of the function without recovery of the destroyed area of the brain demonstrated that the function was now based on a different collection of neuronal modules."[111] Neurons connect differently after the trauma has been addressed and processed. After memory reconciliation, when the neurons are activated, they respond to the same stimulus, and "connect preferentially to form "neuronal ensembles," hence the mantra from Kris Wu who says, "Neurons that fire together wire together."[112] When the painful trauma story finally has a beginning, middle and end, the person feels, thinks, and behaves differently. Once memory reconciliation has happened, the trauma event can be integrated into their life story. During art-making reflections, these integrations, created as phenomena and then written down as reflections, become instrumental in the integration process. Mark Freeman explains, "When it comes to writing about the personal past, of course, the issues at hand become that much more complicated. The inchoate [or developing new] narrative wrought via memory will become codified, solidified; a second order narrativization will take place. "Perspectives are altered by the fact of being drawn."[113]

---

[111] Bruce E. Wexler. *Brain and Culture: Neurobiology, Ideology, and Social Change.* (Cambridge, Mass: Bradford Books, 2006), 28. https://search-ebscohost-com.prov.idm. oclc.org/login.aspx?direct=true&db=nlebk&AN=156966&site=ehost-live.

[112] How Neurons That Wire Together Fire Together. Dec 23, 2021. https://neurosciencenews. com/wire-fire-neurons-19835/ Yue Kris Wu, Friedemann Zenke (2021) Nonlinear transient amplification in recurrent neural networks with short-term plasticity eLife 10:e71263.

[113] Mark Freeman, "Telling Stories: Memory and Narrative." In *Memory: Histories, Theories, Debates* 263–78. Fordham University Press, 2010. http://www.jstor.org/stable/j. cttlc999bq.22. Accessed on Sat, 29 Jul 2023 00:45:49

MEMORY INTEGRATION REQUIRES
THERAPEUTIC SAFETY

Important to the success of the therapeutic process, memory, and self-identity integration, is the fact that trauma memory-reprocessing can only happen if a person feels safe. Secure attachments in relationships make people feel safe. Bonnie Badenoch says, "A safe and secure attachment relationship is an essential foundation for experientially focused trauma treatment approaches."[114] Stephen Porges elaborates that "The human need to be social supplants other survival needs beyond the most primitive needs of oxygen, food, water and physical safety. Social isolation is a powerful disrupter of human behaviour and physiological health… These responses and this sequence are encoded in our genes."[115] In the context of implicit and explicit memory formation and meaning-making during therapy, Badenoch elaborates,

> As we move into close contact with one another, something sometimes happens that can't be defined. The space between seems to hold deepening sense of meaning, expanding vistas of compassion, co-suffering of great intensity at times, and then, often quite suddenly, where the two worlds meet…the door is round and open,… What happens next is as individual as a fingerprint: an expanded sense of oneness with other, a movement toward action on behalf of those in need, the feeling of being held by the Divine, an experience of stillness spreading throughout the body. There is always a sense of something larger, deeper than words unfolding, touching both people in this sacred space between.[116]

---

[114] Bonnie Badenoch. *The heart of trauma: Healing the embodied brain in the context of relationships.* (W.W. Norton & Company, 2018),1.

[115] Stephen Porges in Bonnie Badenoch. *The heart of trauma: Healing the embodied brain in the context of relationships.* (W.W. Norton & Company, 2018), iii.

[116] Bonnie Badenoch. *The heart of trauma: Healing the embodied brain in the context of relationships.* (W.W. Norton & Company, 2018), 3.

This relationship can be seen as an I-Thou relationship where the accountability partner respects and values the humanity of the person who is doing the therapy. Paul Ricoeur explains, "The selfhood of oneself implies otherness to such a degree that one cannot be thought of without the other, that instead, one passes into the other."[117] The selfhood in a relationship with a trusted other happens through the stories we tell of ourselves to the other. Ricoeur argues that people become self-aware of their own identity through narratives. These narratives, when shared, allow self-awareness of personhood because the person experiences and understands that there is an 'other.' The other in the therapeutic process is the accountability partner that you as a reader will choose to engage with before you commence with the trauma processing, as explained in the last chapter. Accountability partners serve the role of a witness to the narrative and the therapeutic processing that will happen over time. Once self-integration has happened, the believer who has reconnected with herself can then rekindle a fresh relationship with the Lord and others. In that way, they can engage with life in a meaning-filled capacity again. This self-integration implies a holistic integration of worldview, how people interact with others, the world, and ultimately with God.

SELF-IDENTITY AND PERSONHOOD CONFIGURATION

Theologian Cherith Fee Nordling describes personhood through the lens of the Trinity: "The Christian story assumes that human being and personhood reflect a prior Reality – the Triune God – through whom humanity derives its being, personhood, identity, and purpose as divine image-bearers."[118] As a believer, I agree with this stance. After all, I am convinced that God himself is to be the blueprint of our personhood. Sociologist Anthony Giddens argues that "Each person has a narrative and a life biography that constitutes the foundation of his or her identity; it is an ongoing activity and something that

---

[117] Paul Ricoeur, *Oneself as Another Translated by Kathleen Blamey.* (The University of Chicago Press. Chicago and London.1992) 3.
[118] Nordling as quoted in T. Larsen & D.J. Treier. Eds. *The Cambridge Companion to Evangelical Theology.* (Cambridge University Press, 2007), 65.

is negotiated through social interaction with others."[119] He explains that identity is never totally fixed but continually adjusted through the telling and re-telling of our stories. According to him, identity formation depends on people's capacity to maintain an ongoing narrative about their story. If true, it implies that when a traumatized person creatively integrates the painful experience into their own narrative, the trauma itself will serve a function in the formation of a new dimension in self-identity. In addition, Giddens suggests, "Identity has to be routinely created and sustained in the reflexive activities of the individual."[120] After trauma these reflexive activities can become destructive and empathetic therapeutic interventions to prevent negative identity fragmentation must happen to assist us in new and healthy identity formation.

Trauma does not only injure our self-identity, but because people then often question their relationship with God after trauma, for believers, traumatic experiences can consequently also result in a tarnished Imago Dei. That is why we as the Christians must rely heavily on Holy Spirit's presence to support self-identity and personhood reconfiguration after traumatic emotional wounding and injury happened to us. When you invite Holy Spirit to be present as the ultimate healer during your therapeutic reflection, the intervention accompanied by *poiesis* has the potential to be transformative so that personhood and self-identity integration become nothing less than miraculous. What can be more wonderful than experiencing the supernatural transformative work of the Holy Spirit in action in your life? Relying on Holy Spirit during the season you work through trauma has many benefits. Ricoeur explains and says in the moments when the self and another connect, "One passes into the other."[121] This implies that when the person of the Holy Spirit is present during times of intense processing—that inherently pursues restoration of your self-identity and personhood—the processing becomes consecrated and can be seen as a 're-birthing,' akin to the

---

[119] Giddens, Anthony. 1991. Modernity and Self-Identity. Self and Society in the Late Modern Age. Stanford: Stanford University Press.1991), 32.
[120] Ibid., 54.
[121] Paul Ricoeur, *Oneself as Another*. Translated by Kathleen Blamey, (The University of Chicago Press. Chicago and London. 1992), 3.

moments of conception. Ricoeur's exploration of the discovery of self-identity concerning the Lord is profound. He states,

> Because he maintains me in existence, God confers on the Certainty of myself the permanence that it does not hold in itself. The strict contemporaneousness of the idea that God and the idea of myself, considered from the angle of the power to produce ideas, makes me say that "just the idea of myself [the idea of God] was born and produced with me when I was created. Better: the idea of God is in me as the very mark of the author upon his work, a mark that assures the resemblance between us. … this likeness… by the same faculty through which I perceive myself. [122]

When God reveals himself to in-dwell the person by his Spirit, it becomes a sacred space, a holy moment.

THE BELIEVER'S IDENTITY WHEN PROCESSING THEIR TRAUMA STORY

For you as a believer, living faithfully in the world implies that your self-identity is solidly integrated with your identity in Christ. Commitment to a life worth living necessitates clarifying your worldview, ways of knowing, and your ontological reality of our world. Doing this results in a person who, according to David Entwistle, not only "Has a more complete intellectual picture of the world, but additionally a more faithful way of living in the world."[123] Entwistle explains that our worldview *Weltanschauung*/confessional vision is defined as "A window through which [we] view the world, framed by the assumptions and beliefs [that] colour what [we] see." [124]

---

[122] Ibid., 33.

[123] David, N. Entwistle, *Integrative Approaches to Psychology and Christianity. An Introduction to Worldview Issues, Philosophical Foundations, and Modalities of Integration.* 3rd ed. (Cascade Books. Eugene, Oregon,2015), 269.

[124] Ibid., 250.

He states that "A worldview frames the backdrop through which we view all dimensions of reality," and says it is, "The mechanisms through which much of human behaviour is mediated. When we move into the realm where we address our emotional wounding, we enact our beliefs about how things should be."[125] When you decide to focus on the workings of God's world, your worldview will provide insight into how you facilitate and understand your behaviour during trauma and when you process it.

The fundamental cornerstone of our worldview is the belief that God is the Creator of all things. He is the only God, Father of all, the great I AM, omnipotent, almighty, and everlasting. This underwrites Anselm of Canterbury's ontological argument about God as the greatest possible being. God simultaneously exists and continues to manifest as an idea in the human mind and our understanding. "So, it is true that there exists something than which nothing greater can be thought, that it cannot be thought of as not existing. And you are this thing, O Lord our God."[126] In reflection on this ontological manifesto, let us draw from Clive S. Lewis who, after he explained the death and resurrection of Jesus, argues as follows,

> Jahweh is the God of nature, her glad Creator. It is He who sends rain into the furrows till the valleys stand so thick with corn that they laugh and sing. The trees of the wood rejoice before Him and His voice causes the wild deer to bring forth their young...On the other hand, Jahweh is clearly not a Nature-God...He is not the soul of Nature, nor any part of Nature. He inhabits eternity: He dwells in a high and holy place: heaven is His throne, not his vehicle, earth is his footstool, not his vesture... He is 'God and not man' His thoughts are not our thoughts.[127]

---

[125] Ibid., 250.

[126] Anselm quoted in McGrath, A. E. *Christian Theology an Introduction,* 6th Ed. (John Wiley & Sons Ltd. Oxford. The U.K, 2017), 56.

[127] C.S Lewis, *Miracles. A Preliminary Study. Geoffrey Bles* (The Centenary Press. London January 1, 1947), 138,139.

To be clear, relating to the story of creation while you address the trauma, we do not confess faith *in* creation, or the phases of creation, as a blueprint for emotional healing. We also believe God as Creator stands apart from His creation. Informing our worldview and theological anthropology, we hold onto a Christian ontology, solidly based on the foundational principles of the Apostle's Creed, which declares:

> I believe in God the Father almighty, creator of heaven and earth, and belief in Jesus Christ, his only Son, our Lord, who was conceived from the Holy Spirit and born of the Virgin Mary, who suffered under Pontius Pilate, was crucified, died, and was buried, descended into hell, rose again from the dead on the third day, ascended into heaven and is seated at the right hand of God the Father almighty, who will come again to judge the living and the dead. I believe in the Holy Spirit, the holy Catholic Church the communion of saints, the forgiveness of sins, the resurrection of the body, and the life everlasting. Amen.[128]

Further to this, we hold to the Trinity where Father, Son, and Holy Spirit are separate, but also One. Irenaeus of Lyons declares: "This is the rule of our faith, the foundation of the building, and what supports our behaviour, God the Father uncreated...The Word of God, the Son of God, our Lord Jesus Christ...the Holy Spirit."[129] The bedrock of addressing trauma through this creative lens, therefore, lies in a reality with God seen as the Alpha, God as the beginning, and God in the beginning. Also, God as Sustainer in the middle, and God, as Omega, at the end. The eternally Triune God who is always in community, continually in a relationship. Peterson explains it well when he says, "God as he reveals himself to us [as]Father, Son, and Holy Spirit ... is triply personal, empathetically personal, unrelenting personal."[130] I

[128] Faith Alive Christian Resources, Christian Reformed Church. *Our Faith, Ecumenical Creeds, Reformed Confessions and Other Resources* (Grand Rapids, Michigan, 2013), 13.
[129] A.E. McGrath. Ed. *The Christian Theology Reader.* 5th ed. (Chichester: Wiley Blackwell, 2017), 157.
[130] Eugene, H. Peterson, *Practice Resurrection: A Conversation on Growing Up in Christ* (Spiritual Theology #5: Eerdmans, 2010),198.

believe God is omnipresent. There is no place He cannot reach; He is the One, the only one God. Stanley Grenz explains, "God is not merely our personal God. The God we know in Christ is [also] the God of the whole world."[131]

With God as *the Creator* of heaven and earth, how we as believers come to understand why creation came into existence, resonates with the belief that the ultimate purpose of creation—as introduced in Genesis 1—was Jesus Christ as the origin and goal of creation. "For in him, [Christ] all things in heaven and on earth were created, things visible and invisible, all things were created through him and for him" (Colossians 1:16). Similar to when creation was explained in the story of Genesis, where God spoke the word, and He created, during therapeutic reflections you can therefore surrender in faith to God, trusting that He, who began a good work in you, is also able to complete and restore what needs to be restored.

We directly and indirectly experience that the cosmos is constantly in flux, and that humanity is bound to suffer trauma. Daily images of violence, wars, natural catastrophes, school shootings, genocides, and refugees fleeing for their lives with little children in hand bombard our news media. Posts on social media haunt us even in the privacy of our homes, and on our phone screens. The effects of trauma are felt everywhere, and Christians have not been promised that they will escape suffering either, instead,

> "Servants, be submissive to your masters, with all fear, not only to the good and gentle, but also to the harsh. For this is commendable, if because of conscience toward God one endures grief, suffering wrongfully, for what credit is it if, when you are beaten for your faults, you take it patiently, this is commendable before God. For to this you were called, because Christ also suffered for us, leaving us an example, that you should follow His steps" (1 Pet 2:18-20).

---

[131] Stanley Grenz, *Created for Community*. 3rd ed. (Baker Academic, Grand Rapids, 2014), 9.

THE ROLE OF THE HOLY SPIRIT DURING THERAPEUTIC ARTMAKING REFLECTIONS

Anticipating that suffering is inescapable and often unmerited, how can believers begin to address their trauma? When pain stories result in trauma wounding, we can hold faith in the ever-present God who manifests in all seasons and dimensions of suffering and pain. How does God manifest and what role does Holy Spirit play when people invite him to be present when they engage with trauma processing? According to Yves Congar, the Christian can only fully actualize as a human when the Holy Spirit shows up in their lives. He says, "To be a Christian, the source of which in us is the Holy Spirit, satisfies in a radical way our quest to be fully human." He explains, "The Holy Spirit is that active presence in us of the Absolute who, at one and the same time, deepens our interior life by making it vibrant and welcoming and puts us in communion with others: the Spirit is what requires and is the means of communication. Yes, we are indwelt." [132] When indwelt by Holy Spirit, hence being secure in our self-other identity, it becomes possible to encounter deeply harmonious relational experiences with others, Congar says. "We can experience an I-Thou relationship not only horizontally, with a human partner, but also vertically, with that partner who is one and the same time infinitely beyond and more intimate than our deepest self."[133]

So, during Lectio Divina meditations and reflective art-making, when you invite Holy Spirit to manifest Himself creatively in the transformative therapeutic process, Holy Spirit can restore and create anew in your life, even after you have experienced chaos and pain. Because, as in the beginning, God is still the Creator of all things beautiful. "In the beginning, God created the heavens and the earth" (Genesis 1:1). Moreover, "By faith, we understand the worlds were prepared by the word of God so that what is seen was made from things that were not visible" (Hebrews 11:13). Daniel Horan says,

---

[132] Yves Congar *The Spirit of God: Short Writings on the Holy Spirit.* (Washington, D.C.: Catholic University of America Press, 2018), 38. https://search-ebscohost-com.prov.idm. oclc.org/login.aspx?direct=true&db=nlebk&AN=1680073&site=ehost-live
[133] Ibid., 39.

"The Spirit is dynamic, unpredictable, immediate, creative, empowering, and life-giving. In the words of the Nicene Creed, the Spirit is vivifican-tem, vivifier or life-giver. This designation refers to creation not just at the beginning of time but continuously: the Spirit is the unceasing, dynamic flow of divine power that sustains the universe, bringing forth life.[134]

This means that Holy Spirit is not far away, but ever-present, also during therapeutic artmaking reflections. Spirit is not a ghost that can't be detected or acknowledged. Clark Pinnock says, "The Spirit is not a numinous power hovering above the cosmos, but a person living in and permeating people in various life situations and specific contexts addressing the needs of the world."[135] Still related to the context of your trauma processing, facilitating space for Holy Spirit to minister grace when you have experienced trauma does not depend on your competency, but it is the power of God's Spirit at work in the given moment. We can focus, as Clark Pinnock says, "Not on the quality …but on the power of God at work in and through [you]."[136] This will release you from the need to 'perform' or strive to achieve some form of excellence in your artmaking. While proceeding with the artmaking directives, you can depend on Holy Spirit to guide the work you are doing. Interestingly is the fact that this reliance on Holy Spirit aligns with what Pinnock explains the function of the church is in relation to the Holy Spirit's dealings in the world: "The church rides the wind of God's Spirit like a hawk endlessly and effortlessly circling and gliding in the summer sky. It ever pauses to wait for impulses of power to carry it forward."[137]

The role of Holy Spirit during the therapeutic processes you will engage with when you address your trauma story, can further be seen as that of a paraclete. In Greek, we read the word as *paraklētos* which is

---

[134] Daniel P Horan, The Holy Spirit. *National Catholic Reporter.* 3/3/2023, Vol. 59 Issue 11, 17.

[135] Clark H. Pinnock, A Review of Veli-Matti Käelieli-Matti Kärkkäinen's Pneumatology: The Holy Spirit in Ecumenical, International, and Contextual Perspective (Grand Rapids: Baker Academic, 2002),7.

[136] Ibid.,114.

[137] Ibid., 114.

widely translated as comforter, intercessor, interpreter, advocate or the more favoured translation, *helper*. Jesus introduces Holy Spirit and what Spirit will do as follows: "And I will pray the Father and He will give you another Helper, that He may abide with you forever – The Spirit of truth, … but you know Him for He dwells with you and will be in you…. But the Helper, the Holy Spirit, whom the Father will send in My name, He will teach you in all things, and bring to your remembrance all things that I said to you." (John 14: 16 – 26). Brian Gaybba argues that Spirit is *another* Paraclete. The first one was Jesus who acted as a Paraclete to his disciples during his time on earth. When Christ left for heaven, he prayed to the Father and becomes the Giver of Spirit to his people. "The Spirit is how Jesus *himself* will continue to be present to them…. No two presences but the same presence is involved."[138] Gaybba concludes, "God is present through the presence of Christ. For just as during his lifetime Jesus was God's Word made flesh, God's image in the world, the one in whom people could see the Father (see John 1:14, 14:9) so too the risen Lord's presence to his people is God's presence to them."[139] This means that when you invite the Holy Spirit into your therapeutic reflections, you can expect to be guided by Him. Spirit will assist you with wisdom and in love, the same way Jesus did it for his disciples. In this way, you can encounter the sweet presence of Holy Spirit to comfort you during this season of difficulty and emotional suffering.

According to Gaybba and relating to the doctrine of Pneumatology, the difference between the Spirit's actions in the Old and the New Testament is that in the New Testament, everything that builds God's people—no matter how ordinary it may be—can be seen as a gift of the Spirit. In the Old Testament, everything the Spirit did, was to prepare people for the day when Christ would come. In the New Testament, the Spirit abides with Christ, where God's Spirit is "not to be found simply in the spectacular, but rather in every act of love. In fact, love, and not the spectacular, is clearly seen as *the* sign of the Spirit's presence. God is love, as 1 John 4:16 put it, and therefore it makes sense that the sign

---

[138] Brian Gaybba, *The Spirit of Love* (Geoffrey Chapman Theology Library, London, 1987), 23.
[139] Ibid., 25.

of God's presence is love."[140] We can take joy in the reality that Holy Spirit is and remains sympathetic to teach us in our life situations and the circumstances we are in right now. Daniel Horan describes the Holy Spirit as a pure gift, "Who draws close to us in our own imperfection, creatureliness and messiness—as the *ruach Elohim* ("breath/spirit of God") does with the *tohu wavo-hu* (chaos, disorder, void) of creation in the opening verses of Genesis."[141]

TRAUMA AND SIN

Previously I explored the theological and psychological roots of narrative and personhood. But it is also important to investigate the relationship between trauma, sin, personhood, and how processing your trauma effectively can support restoration with God if there is sin present in your life. Ray Anderson argues that humans are "creaturely beings" created by God.[142] Further to this, he explains that the *Imago Dei*—God's own self-actualization—and his care for humankind, was altered and changed when sin invaded God's creation. The Protestant Reformers who understood the *Imago Dei* in its relational terms agreed that the identity and image of human beings were deformed as the result of humanity's fall from glory because of sin.[143] That is why, St Augustine, the bishop of Hippo (354 – 430 AD.) prayed, "You have made us for

---

[140] Brian Gaybba, *The Spirit of Love* (Geoffrey Chapman Theology Library, London, 1987), 27.

[141] Daniel P Horan, *National Catholic Reporter*. 3/3/2023, Vol. 59 Issue 11, 17.

[142] Ray Anderson, *On Being Human: Essays in Theological Anthropology* (Wipf & Stock Publishers, 2010), 37.

[143] Genesis 3:6-24. And when the woman saw that the tree *was* good for food, and that it *was* pleasant to the eyes, and a tree to be desired to make *one* wise, she took of the fruit thereof, and did eat, and gave also unto her husband with her; and he did eat. [7]And the eyes of them both were opened, and they knew that they *were* naked; and they sewed fig leaves together, and made themselves aprons. [8]And they heard the voice of the LORD God walking in the garden in the cool of the day: and Adam and his wife hid themselves from the presence of the LORD God amongst the trees of the garden. [9]And the LORD God called unto Adam, and said unto him, Where *art* thou?...Therefore the LORD God sent him forth from the garden of Eden, to till the ground from whence he was taken. 24 So he drove out the man; and he placed at the east of the garden of Eden Cherubims, and a flaming sword which turned every way, to keep the way of the tree of life.

yourself, and our hearts are restless until they rest in Thee."[144] Human beings, created within the context of the relational *Imago Dei*, as seen in Genesis, are intrinsically incomplete until they find their proper *telos*, of completion and goal, which is external to themselves, in God. Sin implies that people have missed God's perfect purpose and goal for their lives through what they think, do and say. Our purpose can only be fulfilled in its totality if we are completely surrendered to God's purpose for our lives. When humanity failed to do that, sin entered our world and our existence. Hence, we live fractured lives that can only be fully restored through accepting Christ's redemptive work on the Cross.

In pursuit of an answer to a complicated and relevant question about humanity and the brokenness of this world, Bonhoeffer explores the question from a Christian anthropological perspective:

> The question of why evil exists is not theological, for it assumes that it is possible to go behind the existence forced upon us as sinners. If we could answer it, then we would not be sinners. We could make something else responsible...The theological question does not arise about the origin of evil but about the real overcoming of evil on the Cross; it asks for the forgiveness of guilt, for the reconciliation of the fallen world.[145]

A strong sense of self and an integrated self-identity is important if you want to engage with life, experience safety, and encounter trust. Bonhoeffer's view on overcoming evil through the Cross lifts the burden of perpetual shame and guilt and assists us in our understanding that believers can anchor their identity in Christ instead of sin and evil. He recognizes and accepts evil does exist but cautions that we should not linger or hold people to it or to the wrong that has happened. Instead, we are reminded that people are more than mere beasts. In Genesis 1:26 – 27 we encounter the *Imago Dei* of humanity as creatures who were created by God in His image to rule over all the earth and all creatures.

---

[144] Ray Anderson, *On Being Human: Essays in Theological Anthropology* (Wipf & Stock, 2010), 65.

[145] D. Bonhoeffer, Schöpfung und Fall /*Creation and the Fall Temptation. Two Biblical Studies.* 2nd ed. (Touchstone, 1959).

Bonhoeffer recommends we see people and accept them in their suffering, help them repent and seek forgiveness, and overcome through Christ who can reconcile them with God to experience restoration. He proposes that we look at God first, because "The Christian story does not [merely] start with "the phenomenon of a human being as a 'societal, individual, or even a theological construct.' It starts with God… [It] assumes that human being and personhood reflect a prior Reality – the Triune God – through whom humanity derives its being, personhood, identity, and purpose as divine image-bearers.[146] When people's story amalgamates with God's Divine narrative for them, their story becomes a glorious narrative of overcoming the tragedy of sin.

Simultaneously, it is also a story of not knowing the beginning or end. It is a constantly evolving story that engages with new meaning-making, including meaning-making about experienced traumas. Bonhoeffer says humanity's story is about reconciliation and restoration. It is a 'middle' story. He expands, "Man no longer lives in the beginning - he has lost the beginning. Now he finds he is in the middle, knowing neither the end nor the beginning, yet knowing that he is in the middle, coming from the beginning and going towards the end. He sees that his life is determined by these two facets, and he "knows only that he does not know them."[147] This in-between story does not affect our identity in Christ, instead, it cements us into God's story for us.

Regarding our self-identity, John Calvin implores that to know who we are as human beings, we first need to understand God. He believes a relationship with God is imperative for self-insight and argues that we will not know what it means to be human without God's self-revelation. He states, "Without knowledge of God, there is no knowledge of self."[148] We must assume that if Calvin's condition for full self-integration and

---

[146] Ray Anderson, Ray, *On Being Human: Essays in Theological Anthropology* (Wipf & Stock Publishers, 2010), 65.
[147] D. Bonhoeffer, *Creation and the Fall Temptation. Two Biblical Studies,* 2nd ed. (Touchstone, 1937).
[148] John Calvin, *Institutes of the Christian Religion, Book 2.* (Calvin Institutes II,1536). https://www.ccel.org/ccel/calvin/institutes.html.26 St. Anselm in David, N. Entwistle, *Integrative Approaches to Psychology and Christianity. An Introduction to Worldview Issues, Philosophical Foundations, and Modalities of Integration,* 3rd ed. (Cascade Books. Eugene, Oregon, 2015), 89.

self-awareness is correct, then, when we as believers proceed to process our trauma wounding, which is mostly because of sin, if not our own, then that of the *other*, we must avail ourselves to get to know God better throughout the process.

To conclude, story and narrative are part of human existence. To make sense of the world we live in and how we relate as individuals to the Lord, others, and the communities we are part of, we create stories and images about our experiences which are then stored as memories. These memories become embodied, and we then live storied lives. When trauma caused by sin shatters our safety and security, the narrative and eventuality of our memories are no longer the same. Typically, trauma sufferers experience the world as a dangerous and lonely place. A new fragmented narrative involuntarily presents itself whenever the person is triggered by an event or image that reminds her of the trauma. Because the trauma story does not have a beginning or an end, the traumatized person's life experience is in a perpetual state of unrest and emotional pain, with fragmented and unintegrated personal narratives. In that way we can lose our sense of destiny and withdraw from intimate relationships and the world; Additionally, believers, when traumatized, begin to doubt their relationship with God. This finally results in a severed self-identity and personhood. A trauma narrative occupies the deeply traumatized person's entire existence. Very often, efforts to escape, such as through substances or destructive behaviour patterns, further perpetuate the fragmentation of self and personhood.

For trauma to be processed, you must learn to trust again. This implies that you must be open and willing to rediscover your identity and learn anew who God intended you to be. Embracing your core beliefs is part of this process. Your self-identity as a believer must be solidly integrated with who you are in Christ. Informing your worldview, I encourage you to take hold of the Christian belief system again. We strengthen our faith when we acknowledge that we exist and have our being because of who God is. Revisiting principles around His character and celebrating the cosmos He has created will assist in this pursuit. Reflecting on God's love for his creation and creatures will inform your artmaking. While you are processing the trauma, and working through your emotional injuries, you can hold onto the reality of the Trinity, the omnipotent God, who stands apart from His creation, inhabits eternity, but remains relationally involved in the lives of his people through His Holy Spirit.

Even though sin and evil are present and no one in the world is exempt from suffering, we can still work through our pain and suffering. When you invite Holy Spirit to be present, you will be guided through the darkness of pain and misery. Allowing for time to process your trauma story and engage with art-making as an aide for your reflections will help you re-tell the pain story from a different perspective. When that happens, the agony is no longer hidden, it is out in the open. Through this prayerful and creative process, you will regroup fragmented memories into new narratives and incorporate the story of trauma into a completed story. In that way, you will experience a new life narrative with a conclusion that will provide an integrated self-identity and personhood. Yes, it is possible to engage effectively in the world; You can attempt healthy relationships with yourself, others, and the Lord. The Spirit, as the Helper, sent by Jesus Christ, makes this possible.

CHAPTER

ART THERAPY AS A PSYCHOTHERAPEUTIC APPROACH

Using creative therapeutic art-making directives to process trauma is foundational to the GENESIS approach for trauma processing in this book. This necessitates why we need to spend some time around what therapeutic art is, and in essence what art therapy as a therapeutic approach looks like. People familiar with the therapeutic benefits of artmaking might not be interested in this chapter, and that is ok. But for those who want to know more and ask why therapists use art to process trauma, the answer lies in therapists' longing to help their clients process painful narratives for meaning-making while they engage with therapeutic art-making. Judith Rubin suggests, "Art is the therapy… and the very foundation of art therapy is *art* itself. Without that basis, there would be no possibility of the discipline."[149] Therapeutic art-making, when used as art reflections assists people towards healthy life-integration. This chapter therefore explores art therapy as the preferred way and approach of how trauma processing is administered. I will examine the story of art therapy through the lens of *poiesis*, which, to re-iterate, is an activity in which a person brings something into being that did not exist before. *Poiesis* in art therapy brings forth images or

---

[149] J.A. Rubin, Editor. *Approaches to Art Therapy. Theory and Technique.* 3rd.ed. Routledge, 2016.),18.

phenomena as an observable fact, occurrence, or thing, for the purpose of meaning-making. I will review the history and development of art therapy over time, current research on its validity in trauma treatment, and explore art therapy's philosophical roots. Further to this, I examine how art therapy is implemented in praxis and include perspectives on art therapy from my theological perspective, where I see theology as, in the words of William Aines, "the teaching [doctrina] of living to God" because Christ has *the words of eternal life* (John 6:68)."[150]

WHAT IS ART THERAPY

Art therapy is a synergistic psychotherapeutic approach with empirical research demonstrating its effectiveness in trauma treatment.[151] The modality arrived at the height of the psychoanalytic era. Although founded on psychoanalytic and psychodynamic techniques, art therapy evolved as a hybrid modality within the egalitarian revolution towards the post-modern era. With its holistic paradigm, art therapy has incorporated psychodynamic, humanistic, systemic, contemplative, cognitive and neuroscience principles in its playbook. This all-inclusive approach developed when art therapists, aware that talk therapy is not always suitable for all people, fused evidence-based psychotherapeutic principles with verified neurobiological frameworks. Referring to art therapy as a synergistic or a hybrid therapeutic approach, Chris Wood defines it as a discipline "situated in-between disciplines such as psychiatry, social work, special education, and psychotherapy."[152] He

---

[150] William Ames, *The Marrow of Sacred Divinity, Drawne Out of the Holy Scriptures, and the Interpreters thereof, and brought into Method* (London: Edward Griffin for John Rothwell at the Sun in Pauls-Church-yard. 1643.), 77.

[151] Camic, (2008); Staricoff & Loppert, (2003) in E. Macri, & C. Limoni. (2017) Artistic activities and psychological well-being perceived by patients with spinal cord injury. *The Arts in Psychotherapy* 54, 1–6. And Schouten, K. A., Gerrit J. de Niet, Knipscheer, J. W., Kleber, R. J., & Giel J. M. Hutschemaekers. (2015). The Effectiveness of Art Therapy in the Treatment of Traumatized Adults: A Systematic Review on Art Therapy and Trauma. *Trauma, Violence & Abuse*, 16(2), 220–228. Accessed January 24, 2023, https://doi.org/10.1177/1524838014555032.

[152] Chris Wood, C. ed., *Navigating Art Therapy. A Therapist's Companion* (Routledge, 2011), 12.

elaborates on the merging in the approach's methodology and explains that while it is an approach in its own right,

> Art therapy exists in a hinterland. People who inhabit hinterlands speak several languages because they [are] crossing backwards and forwards over different borders. Art therapy also contains knowledge of different languages from various interrelated disciplines. It tends not to have orthodoxy and to be playful where it is doing well.[153]

Robert Gray states, "The majority of art therapists view themselves as eclectic and use more than one type of intervention in combination with art therapy in their treatment plans."[154] The rationale for that is clear: psychotherapy is complex. To facilitate lasting change art therapists must not only have a thorough understanding of the different mental health disorders but also endeavour to develop treatment plans that combine evidenced-based psychotherapy practices with art therapy. There is an increased interest in therapies where medication is used and combined with creative practice and talk therapies. Gray says this combination "Fuse[s] evidence-based psychotherapeutic principles with verified neurobiological frameworks to both bypass and leverage language centres to unlock, process and transform."[155] Different and varied art therapy techniques and applications must be adapted to fit individual clients' needs. This strategy aligns with client-centred practices. Functioning effectively as an eclectic art therapist implies the therapist has a thorough understanding of a wide collection of methodologies and approaches, knows which art mediums will work best for different processing to become possible, and possesses the therapeutic skillset and training to seamlessly switch from one modality to the other without confusing the client. This requires knowledge, intuition, creativity, and a mastery of counselling skills and techniques.[156]

---

[153] Ibid., viii.

[154] Robert P. Gray, *Art Therapy and Psychology. A Step-by-step Guide for Practitioners* (Routledge, 2019), 3.

[155] Ibid.,2.

[156] Canadian Art Therapy Association. https://www.canadianarttherapy.org/membership-levels/#registered.

THE HISTORY OF ART THERAPY

Below is a summary of the timeline of art therapy and its alignment with the history of psychology since the beginning of the 20th century:[157]

1900: Freud and Jung, as psychoanalysts, introduced the conscious and unconscious mind as a discourse for mental health and processing. During this period, art therapists who aligned with the psychoanalysts assessed psychological functioning or diagnosed pathology through art. Therapeutic art was seen as a vehicle for subliminal material and associated anxieties. Jean Davies said, "In Freudian terms, symbols in art are considered to be repressed or sublimated projections, representing urges, drives, or impulses of the ego… In Jungian terms, symbols are viewed within an archetypal framework of opposites alerting the ego to seek wholeness and integration."[158] Art therapists were aware of this stance and accommodated psychotherapies in their practice.

The 1930s: During this period art as therapy became used in mental health institutions. Therapists used art making as a therapeutic tool to help with emotional wellness.

The 1940s: During this period there was a move away from *art as therapy* when *art in therapy*, sometimes known as art psychotherapy, became a therapeutic modality. Psychiatrists, psychologists, and art therapists began using drawings and paintings to replace verbal discussions when it was challenging for patients to talk about their problems or trauma. Subsequently, Margaret Naumburg and Edith Kramer, two art therapy pioneers,

---

[157] Robert P. Gray, *Art Therapy and Psychology. A Step-by-step Guide for Practitioners* (Routledge, 2019),10-14.

[158] B.J. Davis, Ph.D., *Mindful Art Therapy. A Foundation for Practice.* (Philadelphia, London: Jessica Kingsley, 2015), 49 -50.

applied their understanding of the unconscious in their therapeutic art with their patients; hence, art therapy became an official mental health discipline. Notably, when art therapy emerged as an identifiable therapeutic approach, it was Edith Kramer who introduced the idea of *art as therapy*. Kramer and Naumburg employed imagery to explore transference and countertransference, prompt therapeutic discussions, and tap into some unconscious material from their patients. During this period, the *House-Tree-Person Projective* drawing test,[159] developed by psychologist John N Buch (1948), became a standardized projective personality test that is still used.

The 1950s: During these years Behavioural Therapy was developed by American psychologists and psychiatrists in reaction to psychoanalyst methods of working with the unconscious. With a tendency to move towards a more pragmatic approach to the change process, art therapy was consequently marginalized by psychoanalysts. This did not deter Margaret Naumburg, who in 1953 advocated for Art Psychotherapy with a strong focus on 'art in therapy,' namely, *art psychotherapy*. In this approach, patients' unconscious material was uncovered by analyzing the produced artwork.

The 1960s: Cognitive Therapy came to the forefront, mainly to address the single-dimensional limitations of behavioural therapy. Cognitive therapy assisted art therapists to identify logical, linear thinking and rationality. During these years, Humanistic theory

[159] Hammer, Emanuel. *Clinical Application of Projective Drawings.* Springfield: (Charles C Thomas Publisher, Ltd, 1980), 451. https://search-ebscohost-com.prov.idm.oclc.org/login.aspx?direct=true&db=nlebk&AN=476774&site=ehost-live. And: Z. Amod, R. Gericke, and K. Bain. "Projective Assessment Using the Draw-A-Person Test and Kinetic Family Drawing in South Africa." In *Psychological Assessment in South Africa: Research and Applications*, edited by Sumaya Laher and Kate Cockcroft, 375–93. Wits University Press, 2013. https://doi.org/10.18772/22013015782.31.

became a third discipline that impacted art therapy and was subsequently incorporated into the field. "Humanistic therapy opposed the determinism of dehumanizing psychoanalysis and behavioural therapy."[160] Significantly, humanistic therapies and art therapy share the belief that people can heal through self-processing their mental health issues with the therapist as a helper to assist them in that.

The 1970s: Cognitive Behavioural Therapy. During this time Behavioural and Cognitive therapy combined to become a paradigm for evidence-based work to address core beliefs, thinking patterns, emotions, and behaviour. This approach has been widely used for decades and art therapy evolved to incorporate CBT principles into the approach. More recognition for art therapy resulted when many psychologists and counsellors trained in CBT realized that CBT alone was insufficient for holistic integration. They also wanted to include the role of the unconscious in their treatment plans; hence, art therapy became part of the holistic treatment plans necessary to work with clients. Other modalities incorporated during this period include Gestalt Therapy and Positive Psychology.

Art Therapy Today: In 1991 art therapy, including expressive art therapy related to trauma treatment, became part of the general psychotherapy paradigm when Dr. James Gordon created the Center for Mind-Body Medicine in New York. He noted this trauma treatment model included "Experiments with guided imagery, words and drawings, music, and movement."[161]

---

[160] Robert P. Gray, *Art Therapy and Psychology. A Step-by-step Guide for Practitioners* (Routledge, 2019),10.

[161] James S. Gordon, *The Transformation. Discovering Wholeness and Healing After Trauma* (Harper One, 2019), 9.

Phenomenological Art Therapy: In 1995 Mala Betensky pioneered and introduced Phenomenological Art Therapy. This approach assisted people in exploring and finding the deeper meaning of their emotions through expression and meaning-making creative art images. This approach will be explored in detail later in the chapter.

In 2009, Cathy Malchiodi, who advocated for an art-as-therapy approach in trauma treatment, created a series of guidelines for the treatment of trauma and submitted it to the International Society for Traumatic Stress Studies (ISTSS). These guidelines included art therapy, music therapy, dance/movement therapy, various forms of therapeutic writing, and drama therapy.[162] Art-as-therapy was implemented for those who struggle with speech and do not know how to self-express through art. Gray celebrates these developments and states, "As practitioners, we can harness the legacy of last century's psychotherapy frameworks, contemporary brain science, and innate human drives to communicate inner experience and creativity, to deliver powerful, transformational therapeutic experiences."[163]

---

[162] "These ISTSS guidelines underscore how the creative arts therapies often include forms of imaginal exposure, cognitive restructuring, and self-regulation in addressing trauma (Johnson Lahad, & Gray, 2009) ... Since the time the guidelines were published, there has been a shift to incorporate more current brain-body approaches rather than solely cognitive restructuring, exposure therapy, and stress management. Based on current evidence-based and emerging brain-body practices, there are eight key reasons for including expressive arts in trauma intervention: (1) Letting the senses tell the story; (2) self-soothing mind and body; (3) engaging the body; (4) enhancing nonverbal communication; (5) recovering self-efficacy; (6) rescripting the trauma story; (7) imagining new meaning; and (8) restoring aliveness.)" In Malchiodi, Cathy A., *Trauma and Expressive Arts Therapy. Brain, Body, & Imagination in the Healing Process* (The Guildford Press, 2020), 24.
[163] Ibid., 2.

THE MULTIPLICITY OF ART THERAPY

Levine argues the "artist/therapist needs to be situated at the borderline of art and psychotherapy; ideally, they will draw from both fields. They intend to help toward healing, and to create, to heal by creating."[164] When words alone cannot tell the client's whole story, art therapy, with its hybrid approach, addresses and assists people in processing their emotional wounding creatively and therapeutically toward holistic integration. None of the many individual psychological theories, theoretical frameworks or therapeutic approaches can claim to cure all issues. Therefore, authors like Malchiodi, Betensky, Levine, Rubin, Gray, and Allen agree and advocate for art therapists to be trained in a wide array of therapeutic modalities.[165] Following is a summary schema of how art therapy integrates other modalities. This table is derived from Judith Rubin's research on the different approaches to art therapy (See Table 2).

---

[164] Ibid., 6.

[165] Rubin, J., A. Ed. *Approaches to Art Therapy. Theory and Technique.* 3rd ed. (Routledge: Taylor and Francis Group, 2016), 2.

ART THERAPY IN PRAXIS WITH OTHER MODALITIES[166]

TABLE 2

Psycho-dynamic Approach	Analytical Approach	Humanis-tic Approach	Contemplative Approach	Cognitive Approach	Neuro-science Approach	Systemic Approach	Integra-tive Approach
Freudian Psycho-analyses	Jungian art therapy	Gestalt art therapy	Art making as a spiritual path	Cognitive Behavioural Art Therapy	CREATE: Art therapy	Family art therapy	Develop-mental art therapy
Object relations	Archetypes as the core of a personal complex	Person-centred Expressive art therapy	Mindful-ness art therapy	Narrative art therapy in trauma treatment	Relational Neuro-science	IFS Group art therapy: Open groups/ Closed groups	Intermodal expressive therapy Music, Movement
Sublima-tion Mentaliza-tion	Image and symbol/ phenomenon	Positive art therapy	Focussing-oriented art therapy Contemplative Wisdom	Directive Group DBT Group		Non-directive groups Thematic groups Analytic Murals	Somatic Perform-ance art Feminist art therapy Heuristic Art therapy
Art Media	Paints, Drawing materials pastels pencils	Clay	Collages Crafts Books Fibre Found objects Stencils	Carvings: Wood, stone	Design: Techno-logy Photo-graphy	Puppets	Body Music instru-ments Body castings

---

166   Ibid.,71 – 430.

ONGOING ART THERAPY RESEARCH

Bruce Moon, a researcher and professor in art therapy, states that even after nearly forty years as an art therapist, his overwhelming sense about the discipline is that art therapy is constantly reforming itself, "While art therapists continue to embrace the artistic dimension of their identity and use creativity when presenting ideas about the discipline, research in the field must therefore continue."[167] Malchiodi explains that "Current studies in the discipline of art therapy employ a variety of traditional research methodologies to engage with evidence-based research to enhance and lift the profile of art therapy as an effective psychotherapeutic modality."[168] Evidence-based research relating to the value of art therapy as a treatment modality became more prevalent after 2014. This occurred following Caroline Chase and Tessa Daly's research as it relates to transference and countertransference. In their study, they explored how the inner experiences from the unconscious can become conscious and verbal during the therapeutic relationships between the therapist and the client. The results showed the validity and contribution of the psychoanalytical approach in art therapy. According to Gray, Chase and Daly's psychoanalytical art therapy approach must not be confused with Carl Rogers' humanistic and client-centred approach, of which the latter also facilitates a solid therapeutic relationship through interpersonal warmth and empathy.[169] According to Malchiodi, art therapy research in Italy also provided long-awaited evidence-based data. [170] The study was implemented as a meta-analysis of quantitative results and Camic stated its purpose was to evaluate the mental health of patients with spinal cord injuries in a hospital. This research was

---

[167] Moon, B.L. Ph.D., *Art-based Group Therapy. Theory and Practice* (Charles C. Thomas, 2010), 139.

[168] According to Malchiodi there are "[t]hree categories of data capture [of] what is currently understood about art-based approaches: (1) meta-analyses that cull[s] data to identify reparative mechanisms; (2) "value-added" studies that examine art-based approaches in combination with evidence-based approaches; and (3) individual feedback on the impact of arts-based approaches within treatment." In Cathy A. Malchiodi, Ph.D., *Trauma and Expressive Arts Therapy. Brain, Body, & Imagination in the Healing Process* (The Guildford Press, 2020), 21-23.

[169] Ibid.,10.

[170] Ibid., 38-45.

completed "As a result of the growing interest that has been recorded in the relationship between art and health, and … [provided] understanding [on] how art can be used as a tool capable of exerting a positive impact upon human health."[171] The study focused on art therapy as a treatment that supports and complements pharmacological and medical therapies. The therapeutic goal of the research was to assess how stress was reduced during patients' hospital stay, helping patients deal with the impact of hospitalization and ill health and, more generally, by positively affecting levels of individual psychological well-being among patients. The results supported the hypothesis that "Participating in artistic activities when art-as-therapy was implemented, positively affects the psychological well-being of patients with spinal cord injuries."[172] Because of these findings, it was recommended that creative activities be incorporated into the therapeutic services provided by other hospitals in Italy.

Over thirty years (1983 – 2016), Judith Rubin's research about art therapy as an approach brought the realization that, according to her,

> This synergistic discipline has developed sufficiently over the last three decades for its most sophisticated practitioners to be as secure in their *artist* identity as in their *therapist* persona. Art originally meant the visual arts, the terms *expressive arts*, while still evolving, have gained much greater acceptance in recent years…A related development in art therapy over the last few decades has been an increasing level of comfort with the idea of *play*.[173]

According to Catherine Hyland Moon, who studied the impact of different art mediums used during art therapy, the effects of each different medium showed to be variable components of the therapeutic

---

[171] Camic, (2008); Staricoff & Loppert, (2003) in E. Macri, & C. Limoni. (2017) Artistic activities and psychological well-being perceived by patients with spinal cord injury. *The Arts in Psychotherapy* 54, 1–6.

[172] Ibid., 6

[173] J.A, Rubin, Ed. *Approaches to Art Therapy. Theory and Technique.* 3rd ed., (Routledge, 2016), 2,3.

exchange.[174] Hyland Moon cautions that a therapist's lack of knowledge or experience with new materials or emerging technologies may limit clients' access to these materials and media. She recommends that the client's preferred medium take precedence over the therapist's familiarity with an art medium. It is expected that an adequate variety of art supplies should be available for the person to explore when engaging with therapeutic reflections during artmaking. Moon recommends that people should be encouraged and helped to discover materials that work best in their therapeutic processing.[175]

While it proved to be a helpful tool in providing empathic attunement during therapy, another technique that is currently being researched and explored is Edith Kramer's original 'third hand' conceptualization which she introduced in 1986. In this approach, the art therapist acted as an artist to facilitate the patient's art expression. In 2001 Mildred Chapin, while working with suicidal patients in a psychiatric hospital, where the patients were non-responsive to verbal treatments altered this approach by "Involving the art therapist's creation of her own art as a *response* to what the patient presented."[176]

Important to mention in this regard is the distinction between art-based research or ar(t)ography. Shaun McNiff defines art-based research as "The use of artistic expression by the researcher, either alone or with others, as a primary mode of inquiry. It is not just about art as a subject of research, (ar(t)ography, but art as a tool and process of research."[177] For this book, I used a heuristic art therapy inquiry to derive conclusions for the art directives used in Chapter 5.

---

[174] Catherine Hyland Moon, *Materials and Media in Art Therapy. Critical Understanding of Diverse Artistic Vocabularies* (Routledge, Taylor and Francis Group, 2010), 11-14.

[175] Ibid.,14.

[176] M. Chapin & B. Fish, The Therapist as Artist. In J.A, Rubin, Ed. *Approaches to Art Therapy. Theory and Technique.* 3rd ed., (Routledge, 2016), 33-45.

[177] R.W. Prior, Ed. *Using Art as Research and Learning and Teaching. Multidisciplinary Approaches Across the Arts* (Intellect, 2018), xi.

THE EFFECTIVENESS OF ART
THERAPY TO TREAT TRAUMA

Research about the effectiveness of art therapy in trauma treatment delivered some interesting results. In 2015, a team of researchers identified and evaluated the empirical evidence for the efficacy of art therapy for trauma treatment. A systematic review of six comparative studies found a significant decrease in psychological trauma symptoms in three groups, and one study reported "A significant reduction in depression."[178] Janice Lobban's extensive research on the implementation of art therapy in treating veterans and serving armed forces personnel of the United States Army who suffered from Post Traumatic Stress Disorder also provided valuable evidence of positive results of art therapy after severe post-traumatic stress.[179] In addition, Gantt and Greenstone's research results on Narrative Art Therapy (NAT) are fascinating. Informed by neurobiology, Louis Tinnin and Linda Gantt developed NAT over thirty years. Its theoretical principles incorporated research results related to brain mechanisms, clinical observation, and knowledge about instinctual survival strategies. When NAT was utilized as the principal means of processing traumatic events, Tinnin and Gantt's findings successfully identified that the universal stages of traumatic experience are processed in the non-verbal brain and mind. Their research findings resulted in a recommendation for NAT to be investigated as the modality of choice in treating post-traumatic stress disorder and dissociative disorders.[180]

---

[178] Schouten, K. A., Gerrit J. de Niet, Knipscheer, J. W., Kleber, R. J., & Giel J. M. Hutschemaekers. (2015). The Effectiveness of Art Therapy in the Treatment of Traumatized Adults: A Systematic Review on Art Therapy and Trauma. *Trauma, Violence & Abuse*, 16(2), 220–228. Accessed January 24, 2023, https://journals.sagepub.com/doi/10.1177/1524838014555032

[179] J. Lobban, *Art therapy with military veterans: Trauma and the image.* 1st ed; Vol. 1 (Taylor & Francis eBooks A-Z. Routledge, 2018). Accessed January 24, 2023, https://doi.org/10.4324/9781315564197

[180] L. Gantt & L. Greenstone, Narrative Art Therapy in Trauma Treatment in J.A. Rubin, Ed. *Approaches to Art Therapy. Theory and Technique.* 3rd ed. (Routledge, 2016), 353-370.

THE NATURE OF ART THERAPY

Art therapy is, in essence, about the creation of images. Stephen Levine states that "[p]sychology articulates itself in concepts, but the psyche, [or the soul] of a person needs the image to come forth, whatever form the image may come to take, whether in pictures, words, sounds, movements, or scenes. The image allows the psyche to reveal itself in ways that transcend the order produced by rational discourse."[181] Mala Betensky originally introduced the concept of image in phenomenological art therapy. What happens during phenomenological art therapy interventions? According to Gray, "A spontaneous connection occurs between the elements of the [image] and the client's unconscious mind, where the visual image is interpreted by the unconscious as a sensation, a memory, or any number of things that are relevant to the client which then becomes conscious."[182] Cathy Malchiodi, theorist, psychologist, and expressive art therapist, places art therapy in its psychotherapeutic context when she defines it as:

> [T]he purposeful use of visual art materials and media in intervention, counselling, psychotherapy, and rehabilitation; it is used with individuals of all ages, families, and groups. Within the applications of art therapy, there is a continuum of practice ranging from art as therapy, art-making as a reparative, life-enhancing activity [t]o art psychotherapy, the purposeful, integrative application of [art]based intervention within a variety of psychotherapeutic and counselling approaches.[183]

The clear distinctions between when art-in-therapy is implemented versus when art-as-therapy is important when it becomes the focus of

---

[181] Levine, Stephen K. *Trauma, Tragedy, Therapy. The Arts and Human Suffering* (London: Jessica Kingsley Publishers, 2009), 26.

[182] Robert P. Gray, *Art Therapy and Psychology. A Step-by-step Guide for Practitioners* (Routledge, 2019), 12.

[183] Cathy A Malchiodi, *Trauma and Expressive Arts Therapy. Brain, Body, & Imagination in the Healing Process* (The Guildford Press, 2020), 15.

the intervention. Gray states that the art therapist who is also an artist will "Emphasize the healing power of the 'art-as-therapy ' while the psychologist… see it as a tool to facilitate communication throughout unconscious material…some… think in a more contemplative or so-called 'transpersonal way' about art therapy connecting us to a deeper and more meaningful place that reaches beyond us."[184] Summarized, in *art-as-therapy*, artmaking itself, seen as *poiesis*, and using art media to create art is cathartic and healing. Gray reported that research has shown when art-as-therapy is implemented during therapeutic interventions there is "A rise of alpha wave patterns [which]results in a relaxed state of mind or restful alertness. Serotonin levels appear to increase, which alleviates the feeling of depression [and] cortisol levels are reduced. Research has shown that stress is reduced when cortisol levels drop."[185] Gray says, "Art-as-therapy is often implemented with young children and the elderly or with clients who are neurodiverse with intellectual challenges."[186] With art-in-therapy, the process of making art (*poiesis*) becomes the focus of the therapeutic intervention. During the intervention, the therapist observes and inquires about the creative art-making process as well as what the created phenomenon is revealing to the client themselves. Notably, it is not about what the art therapist sees. This principle lies at the heart of phenomenological art therapy. Currently, most art therapists will incorporate both art-as-therapy and art-in-therapy in their practice and believe that both forms belong together because they meaningfully influence each other. Therapists will implement each modality depending on the individual client and their problems. The emphasis of one modality can change from one focus to the other.

[184] Robert P. Gray, *Art Therapy and Psychology. A Step-by-step Guide for Practitioners* (Routledge, 2019),11.
[185] Ibid.,12.
[186] Ibid.,12.

THE PHILOSOPHICAL ROOTS
OF ART THERAPY

Understanding art therapy's relevance in the psychotherapeutic field requires a philosophical exploration of its foundational principles. Stephen Levine attempts a clear and thorough defence of art therapy as part of expressive art therapies, to be a therapeutic modality that can take its place among the world's most well-recognized psychotherapeutic modalities. Levine, an expressive art therapist and theorist, places creativity at the centre of art therapy and the centre of humanity when he states, "The potential for creative existence [is] in each one of us.[187] He argues that the creative act, or *poiesis* - the way Heidegger applied the concept when he borrowed it from the original Greek - is an action by which humankind affirms our humanity and, subsequently, our identity. Levine concludes that when art-making is seen and experienced as *poiesis* during therapeutic interventions, "This creative act, when applied appropriately, makes the psychotherapeutic intervention transformative and becomes, in its essence, an art form as well."[188]

Therapeutic interventions are indeed an art form in itself. During The Enlightenment, a Newtonian epistemology was introduced, which viewed all natural phenomena as subject to scientific principles and laws. The Enlightenment era was also the context in which modern therapy emerged. Researchers agreed that during this period only rational and understandable laws were seen to govern the universe. Sigmund Freud, the founder of psychoanalysis, aligned his worldview with the Newtonian conception of scientific knowledge. Subsequently to this, his views had a significant impact on psychotherapy. In alignment with an epistemology that viewed and explained everything in the context of science and psychotherapy, psychological suffering was consequently understood as a nervous disorder in the nervous system, or "neurosis." This later became the term applied as 'disorders of the imagination.' Moreover, according to Levine, "The task of the medical doctor was then to work toward the elimination of the symptom by curbing the workings

---

[187] Stephen K. Levine, *Poiesis. The Language of Psychology and the Speech of the Soul* 2nd ed. (Palmerston Press, 1992), xvi.

[188] Ibid., 3-4.

of the individual's imagination … Psychotherapy, under the shadow of the Enlightenment's conception of truth as unmediated access to objective reality, became a cure of the imagination."[189] Over time, and after psychotherapy has revealed the power of the imagination in mental life, therapists slowly became aware that the cure for imaginary disorders could not come from purely rational processes alone. Instead, the therapist should see the cure as a 'renovation of the imagination itself.' Levine states that Freud's method of free association, and Jung's concept of active imagination, in its facilitation of a waking state of imaginative potency, showed that "A major part of psychotherapy is the healing *of* the imagination *by* the imagination."[190] Psychotherapy has evolved, and currently, its purpose is no longer to eliminate people's imagination; in its place, Levine says, our therapeutic ideal as therapists is to help people free their imagination, assisting them to live and engage in a more creative way in the world they live. That means that art therapists want to "Rid the imagination of its suffering, its pathology, which takes the form of fantasies that are stereotypical, compulsive, repetitive and destructive of self and others."[191] When Levine sees the need for people's imagination to be freed toward healthy emotional integration, he agrees with Emanuel Kant; the latter considers imagination the essence of the soul. "It is not the image, but the act of imagination that unifies and integrates our experience of the world and of the self."[192] He explains that Kant sees the world and God as non-objective totalities that cannot be known in their essence. We cannot entirely sense God or the world in its fullness, but that does not mean they do not exist. Levine argues that if Kant's theory is correct, the soul is not a psychic entity but the *origin* or *source of experience*. According to him, Heidegger aligns with Kant's idea of the soul and eventually concludes that the human being is essentially creative. Regarding fragmentation and brokenness, Levine uses these two philosophers' thinking to explain that when people come to therapy, they are often experiencing a crisis where they feel fragmented or perceive themselves to be 'falling apart.' During this

---

[189] Ibid., 2.
[190] Ibid., 3.
[191] Ibid., 3.
[192] Ibid., 20.

period of disintegration, "The therapeutic act consists of 'being-with' clients as they go through their suffering. ...It seems we need the help of others to be ourselves. It is essential to realize that the restored self is different from the initial identity."[193] Metaphorically, clay in the hands of the potter remains essentially clay. However, because it is surrendered to the creative process, the moulding will cause the clay to change its shape and be functional. Without the intervention of the potter, it will remain formless and without purpose. Levine states, "Creation depends upon destruction, a willingness to give up a previous pattern and to experiment with a new form. In this sense, all therapy is, in essence, creative."[194] He concludes that humanity's creativity can and should be utilized in the healing and restorative process:

> Would be to God that all the Lord's people were Poets. The dialectic of creativity from innocence to experience and back again requires of us that we descend as poets, as artists, into the lives that we have led, that we recognize and accept our experience of loss and find again the innocence that will restore us to ourselves and enable us to create our world anew."[195]

This reminds me of Moses, who similar to Levine's plea for creative synthesis in therapy, longed for the restoration for God's people to also engage with the Lord healthily and creatively, as expressed in the book of Numbers: "Oh that all the Lord's people were prophets and that the Lord would put His Spirit upon them" (Numbers 11:29). Levine further claims that all expressive arts therapies "Rest on the premise that imagination is the healer. Encouraging the soul to speak in its own way transforms darkness into light, the hidden and concealed into the open, and thus provides insight and release."[196] Levine believes one of expressive arts therapy's foundational principles lies in the idea that the imagination cares for and holds the secrets that can assist towards a cure for the suffering of the human soul. He says, "The therapist attends to

---

[193] Ibid., 22.
[194] Ibid., 22-23.
[195] Ibid., 92.
[196] Ibid.,92.

the suffering of the soul, its psychopathology. The therapist attends to its suffering, pays attention to it, and helps it to show itself, to present itself, to become present." [197]Aligning with this assumption is the idea that the art therapist must assist individuals in being imaginal too. Levine believes the therapist "must be capable of imagining the psyche, of finding and interpreting the images and myths that can let the psyche speak. Otherwise, the soul is imprisoned in the conceptual network of psychological systems; it languishes, flees, or dies."[198]

PHENOMENOLOGICAL PRINCIPLES IN ART THERAPY

We pay close attention to externalized art phenomena that emerge during art-making. Mala Betensky, who holds a phenomenological perspective of art therapy, referred to this as the "thingly thing."[199] This notion aligns with the concept *of the phenomenon*, which is derived from the Greek verb 'to appear' and can be observed and perceived through our mind and senses. Betensky explains, "In its simplistic form, the philosopher Edmund Husserl (1859-1938) saw phenomenology as the essence of all things. He called for "A turn 'to the things' themselves and the investigation of the fullness of subjective experiencing 'things' away from preconceived or inferred theories about them."[200] Stephen Levine clarifies that the phenomenon shows itself to us and recommends that we carefully consider the image when it reveals itself. When that happens, he says, "We need to let the phenomenon speak, help it to name itself, to tell its story...Perhaps there are multiple stories, many discourses, and dialogues."[201] Levine encourages *poiesis* in the context of the phenomenon as the image and way of telling stories and does so by aligning himself with Martin Heidegger's exploration:

[197] Ibid., 27.
[198] Ibid., 96-97.
[199] Mala G. Betensky, *What Do You See? Phenomenology of Therapeutic Art Expression* (London: Jessica Kingsley Publishers, 1995), 3.
[200] Ibid., 3-4.
[201] Stephen K. Levine, *Trauma, Tragedy, Therapy. The Arts and Human Suffering* (London: Jessica Kingsley Publishers, 2009), 25-26.

We know something by shaping it, by giving it a form. Art-making is a way of shaping the truth and 'setting it into a work.' In so doing, we let the truth of what the work points to show itself. When it does, we have the experience of beauty. Beauty is the phenomenon par excellence. It is what happens when we are able to let that which we experience show itself as it is in itself. This explains the power of the arts in our lives and the therapeutic space.[202]

Betensky underwrites an anthropo-philosophical view of humanity as "present-and future-oriented human beings-in-the-world," who are persons and not objects, "Each of them is a phenomenon with ... individually coloured innate qualities and propensities that make their relationships in their worlds highly individual."[203] She states these phenomenological qualities are "Intentionality, experiencing that involves all mental, consciousness self-reflection, a need to create, and the striving for mental and spiritual growth throughout life."[204] In tandem with this belief, she embraces a phenomenological methodology for art therapy with the basic tenets to be:

1. The art production is a phenomenon with its structure
2. The client learns to see all that there can be seen in it
3. The client's verbal description of the work's structure is essential
4. The client connects the artwork with the inner experience.[205]

---

[202] M. Heidegger, 'The Origin of the Work of Art' In *Poetry, Language, Thought* (New York: Harper & Row,1975) in Stephen K. Levine, *Trauma, Tragedy, Therapy. The Arts and Human Suffering* (London: Jessica Kingsley Publishers, 2009), 26.

[203] "Phenomena include visible, touchable, and audible things in the world around us, as well as thoughts and feelings, dreams, memories, fantasies, and all that stems from the human mind or spirit and belongs in the realm of mental experiences. By means of the study of the consciousness, Husserl tried to reduce the perception of phenomena to their essence." Edmund Husserl, Ideas; 1913; 2nd ed. (N. J: Humanities Press,1976) in Mala G. Betensky, *What Do You See? Phenomenology of Therapeutic Art Expression* (London: Jessica Kingsley Publishers, 1995), 3-4.

[204] Ibid., xi.

[205] Ibid.,14-21.

Betensky believes that Phenomenological art therapy should be celebrated as a positive approach. First, it is about the images concerning the individual, who themselves become a phenomenon which perceives, experiences, and interacts with the images. According to this perspective, a person who engages in therapeutic artmaking is then a phenomenon who is coming to new insights about themselves that assist in their striving towards emotional, spiritual, and mental health. About the image: the image, identified as art, is then seen as a universal phenomenon that can be studied during the therapeutic art intervention. People experience images continuously when they dream, through their senses, smell a fragrance, hear music, or read a poem. People see images in their mind's eye when they think about places they have gone to or want to go to when they think about themselves or people they know, love, or hate. Through artmaking, the person who created the art gives these subconscious encounters and images form. When those images receive a form, it is not evaluated by any outside criteria but by what the individual who processes it, senses it to be true for them.

THE APPRECIATION OF IMAGINATION IN ART THERAPY

In alignment with the phenomenological stance, Wilkinson and Chilton argue for viewing art therapy as an inherently positive treatment modality where people can appreciate their imagination. They believe art therapy "Enjoys a natural intersection with flow, creativity and positive emotion [...and] should be a full immersion of mind, body and spirit."[206] The therapeutic idea is to help people by freeing their imagination, assisting them to live and engage more creatively in their world. Pat Allen considers a person's imagination the most important faculty to possess. However, she cautions that imagination can be a person's most excellent resource or a formidable adversary. "[The] imagination is no mere blank slate on which we inscribe our will ...

[206] Wilkinson, R. A., & Chilton, G. Positive Art Therapy: Linking Positive Psychology to Art Therapy Theory, Practice, and Research. *Art Therapy*, (2018):*30* (1), xv -58. Accessed January 2, 2023, https://doi.org/10.1080/07421656.2013.757513

we each have a lifetime of patterns and habits of thought embedded there, based on past experiences. Our expectations of ourselves and the world flow from these patterns."[207] Allen explains, "Art making is a way to explore our imagination and begin to allow it to be more flexible, to learn how to see more options,"[208] and encourages art therapists to clarify for their clients that fear can often stop the imagination before it begins to work for their benefit. Shaun McNiff believes "The practice of imagination requires an ongoing interplay between many different and often contradictory elements. It is a gathering of forces ... images birth one another ... the image opens... the doors to the imagination."[209] Art making conclusively explores the imagination. However, utilizing the imagination for artmaking, McNiff advocates that people must be trained to use their imagination during artmaking by gradually engaging with the flow and the process.[210] In recent years the generic concept of 'Flow' has in itself become a study. For this book, flow is not discussed in the sense of artistic expression but rather in how the therapeutic process continues.

People who create art images for trauma processing must learn to apply awareness and self-awareness while their senses practice the practical application of the imagination. It works effectively if done in a playful and restful manner. Therapeutic art embraces imagination in concert with play. Winnicott, a world-renowned child psychologist who has impacted art therapists' view on the therapeutic space and therapeutic alliance formation, indicates, "Psychotherapy takes place in the overlap of two areas of playing, that of the patient and that of the therapist. Psychotherapy has to do with two people playing together." [211]

---

[207] Pat B. Allen, *Art is a Way of Knowing. A Guide to self-knowledge and spiritual fulfillment through Creativity* (Shambhala,1995), 3.

[208] Ibid., 4.

[209] Shaun McNiff, *Trust the Process* (Shambhala, 1998), 2 – 5.

[210] Ibid., 5

[211] "Winnicott discovered transitional space through play. [He] is always playing even when he is merely present. He never becomes a distant observer outside of the field of play. Rather the therapeutic space is understood as a playground, a place where both patient and analyst are involved. In this space, interpretation cannot come "outside" if there is any interpretation at all. Instead, it must come from within the transitional world in which both analyst and patient play." In Stephen K. Levine, *Poiesis. The Language of Psychology and the Speech of the Soul* 2nd ed. (Palmerston Press, 1992), 33.

Winnicott and Levine explain the importance of play as *an operation of the imagination,* not fantasy. Levine clarifies that therapy revitalizes the imagination and assists in a "Turning-back to an original connection between self and world."[212] To do that, he introduces Winnicott's discovery of the transitional space through the play experience. Levine extrapolates that Winnicott implies "That psychic life is imaginal; we live in the imaginative and playful space of experience."[213] He explains that when therapeutic art interventions occur, the person inevitably engages with imaginative play, where creativity can be released so that integration and healing can occur. People must therefore be encouraged toward playful engagement when they create art. This is important because, in the play, there is no right or wrong in image-creating. Creativity can flow in this in-between, safe, imaginative, and transitional space. The person can discover new insights and truths about their process during imaginative play and creating art images. Then, reflections on the phenomenological image they have made while playing become meaningful and transformative. Allen encourages that when people engage with the imagination playfully, they must be invited to become aware of shapes, colours, textures, and details. Apart from the fact that these elements all constitute art, it acts in a way that evokes different feelings, stirs new memories, and can activate the imagination to make connections as it relates to the therapist's therapeutic process.

When Allen speaks about cultivating a creative and helpful imagination, she promotes mindfulness, even though she is not using the term. Mindfulness is the active component of the mind in meditation, but one does not necessarily need to meditate to be mindful. Davis says, "Mindfulness is about paying attention to how things are in the moment. John Kabat-Zinn (1994) has characterized mindfulness as "Paying attention in a particular way: on purpose, in the present moment, and non-judgmentally."[214] Even though there are different definitions and opinions about mindfulness, when people want to apply a mindful stance during therapeutic art-making, they must be willing to

---

[212] Ibid.,32,33.

[213] Ibid., 33.

[214] Davis, B.J. Ph.D., *Mindful Art Therapy. A Foundation for Practice* (Jessica Kingsley, 2016), 22.

be present at the moment, open, interested, receptive, and fully engaged. Allen argues art is a way of knowing "What it is we actually believe. "[215] She claims to make art, where individuals give form to the images that arise in their mind's eye about their dreams and their everyday lives, including experiences from the past, is a form of spiritual practice through which knowledge of the self can bring self-discovery, -insight, wisdom and, healing.

Advocating for an individual to nurture awareness during therapeutic art interventions, Allen encouraged curiosity, learning to think about different possibilities and inquire about the origin of an image. She believes this will stimulate creative and effective imagination for people to know how and where to apply the images that come to mind during their art-making to gain insight into their process. She says, " Draw these images and welcome them into your life like the long-lost orphans they are…Play with them like old friends… These are the openings to knowing the roots of your creative self." [216] Levine also encourages fostering a healthy imagination. He explains that since its conception, psychotherapy has engaged with the imagination and concludes, "The arts and art-making are rooted in the practices of the imagination."[217] The imaginative and creative engagement with images throughout the therapeutic intervention is the 'tool of the trade' that introduces a new dimension to the therapeutic process. This principle sets the approach apart from all other methods.

Levine insists that people can create art in even their darkest hours. He cites the art of the Holocaust as an example where people's art adequately expressed their darkest emotional suffering. "The creative arts, then, can enter into psychotherapeutic work because art has an inherent capacity to heal the psyche."[218] In addition, he explains that rituals, whether in religious activities or over time, were used to have a cathartic or purifying effect. A Biblical example of this artmaking about ritual and religious activities relates directly to Exodus chapters 25 to

---

[215] Pat B. Allen, *Art is a Way of Knowing. A Guide to self-knowledge and spiritual fulfillment through Creativity* (Shambhala, 1995), 3.

[216] Ibid.,179.

[217] 219 Stephen. K. Levine, *Poiesis. The Language of Psychology and the Speech of the Soul.* 2nd ed. (Palmerston Press, 1992), 3-7.

[218] Ibid., 3-4.

27, where God instructed the Israelites on the design and creation of the Tabernacle. We also read in Exodus 32 how they misappropriate their creative ability by making a golden calf that they could worship. Another example of creative rituals as restorative processes can be found in the second book of Samuel, chapter 6, where David and thirty thousand of his choice soldiers brought back the Ark of the Covenant to Jerusalem.[219] David's use of poetry and song in the Psalms is also a form of *poiesis.*

Levine adds another dimension to art therapy in psychotherapy when he sees the approach as an art form in itself. He argues that psychotherapists function in their practices more like artists than scientists and says, "Unless, of course, science itself is seen as a creative process."[220] He addresses art therapists as artists and encourages them to remain sensitive to their process. He promotes regular engagement with transformative expressive arts to confront and ease their woundedness. Not only should they use artmaking in processing their pain, but he argues that in most cases, the result of their art could also touch the souls of the people who behold their art in a positive and transformative manner. Pat Allen is in total agreement with this stance. She argues that a lifestyle of artmaking, with a purpose and role towards self-integration, sense, and meaning-making is necessary for all people in order "To discover or re-discover and gain insight about their own soul."[221] Rubin, Tinnin and Malchiodi advocate for continuing artmaking, but their focus is on the importance of personal reflection when creating art. Simultaneously, they urge that "Art therapists [must] remain flexible and open to sharpening their skills in other psychotherapeutic modalities as well."[222] Robert Gray says art therapy helps humans "explore who we are."[223] In reflection, this rationale that people must continue their own

---

[219] 2nd Samuel 6:5-13. "Then David and all the house of Israel played music before the Lord on all kinds of instruments of fir wood, on harps, on stringed instruments, on tambourines, on castanets, and on cymbals... And so it was, that when those bearing the ark of the Lord had gone six paces, that he sacrificed oxen and fatted sheep."

[220] Stephen. K. Levine, *Poiesis. The Language of Psychology and the Speech of the Soul,* 2nd ed. (Palmerston Press, 1992), 9.

[221] Ibid., 3.

[222] Rubin, J., A. Ed. *Approaches to Art Therapy. Theory and Technique.* 3rd ed. (Routledge: Taylor and Francis Group, 2016), 2-14.

[223] Robert, P. Gray, *Art Therapy and Psychology. A Step-by-step Guide for Practitioners* (Routledge, 2019), 6.

artmaking and self-processing throughout their lives makes sense. It will be sad if people only meditate and reflect on Scripture when they experience pain in their lives, and not in their daily walk with the Lord.

Metaphors and symbols when revealed through therapeutic art reflections, help people to make connections between emotional and mental processing. It is healing, aesthetically enjoyable and releases creativity. During therapeutic art-making, people take the raw materials of their life and form them into a significant whole. "The self is created out of what we have been by casting forward (projecting) a vision of what we may be."[224]

Art therapy's aesthetic theory encompasses the entire approach. It dynamically informs the conceptual, relational, and meaning-making process during the implementation of the therapy, as well as the processing of the person's process, which art supplies they used, and how well the therapeutic alliance was formed between the person and their accountability partner, who can be a counsellor or a pastoral therapist. During therapeutic art-making the emphasis is on the processing, but there is something to be said of aesthetic satisfaction. When a person has created something that they see as beautiful, they can feel good about it. But, it is important to remember that trauma processing's success has its origins more in the emerging work than in competence related to technical skills. Artmaking encompasses a wide range of art practices, including artwork on or with the body, time-based art, sound art and ephemeral, conceptual, collaborative, participatory, or action-based art."[225] Relevant to aesthetics, however, is always the insight that the artmaking images made during art interventions are not just meant to be aesthetically beautiful. Instead, it concerns the person's image of their process, experience, and emotions about an issue. That, if explored well, is by itself aesthetically beautiful.

---

[224] Stephen K. Levine, *Poiesis. The Language of Psychology and the Speech of the Soul.* 2nd ed. (Palmerston Press, 1992), 4.

[225] Catherine Hyland Moon, Relational Aesthetics and Art Therapy. In J.A. Rubin. Ed. *Approaches to Art Therapy. Theory and Technique.* 3rd ed. (Routledge, 2016), 55.

ART THERAPY CELEBRATES
INDIVIDUALITY

Each person is unique and processes life events instinctively. That is why different modalities and approaches with individual intervention techniques are developed to adapt to people's thinking styles when they engage in therapy. For example, when a person chooses to create art during their trauma processing, they must keep these unique and individual differences in mind and look for several creative art mediums and techniques to explore during the therapeutic interventions. Therapeutic interventions mostly materialize with and without verbal communication.

The influence of art to assist in emotional healing does not originate in a particular art-making technique alone but in the entire creative process. This suggests people must practice developing their imaginative and creative capabilities to think and explore new possibilities to address their situation or problems for positive outcomes. Hogan states, "Metaphors, symbols and the expressive use of art materials combine to create a rich language for self-expression and the opportunity for the translation of strong emotions into a pictorial expression which can be visceral in its intensity."[226] When a person gets stuck by working with one art medium only it often helps to begin working with a new medium. For example, if you have worked with oil pastels for a long time and feel that you are no longer enjoying working with the medium, it often helps to switch from pastels to other paints or experiment working with clay. It is also important to remember that some people can express their feelings through art materials, but others can better express feelings through writing or poetry. Any art medium is welcome during therapeutic art-making. Yes, some do it through drawing, painting, carving, or music, while others do it through movement. All of these must be available during your therapeutic exploration process.

People have different opinions about trauma processing. Cathy Malchiodi, who advocates a brain-body framework for expressive arts therapy, cautions against a stage-by-stage approach to trauma interventions. Her argument is mainly geared to caution against the

---

[226] Hogan, Susan, *Art Therapy Theories. A Critical Introduction* (Routledge, 2016), 1.

continuum of Neuro-developmental Art Therapy (NDAT) and Dance Movement Therapy. She states that "Individuals who experience traumatic events do not neatly progress through universal phases of recovery, nor do they fit into sequential steps when it comes to standardized arts-based procedures. ...[instead] each individual or group has additional, unique responses due to many factors and influences."[227] However, reflecting on trauma that fragments linear engagement, I somewhat disagree with Malchiodi's caution against sequential trauma recovery treatment plans and implementation. Yes, from a neuro-developmental perspective, it is apparent that people cannot recover at the same pace or in the same way. However, it makes sense to me to allow people to process trauma in a step-by-step fashion. Providing traumatized people with the safety of predictability and order during therapeutic interventions helps the affected brain to engage linearly. It also helps with stability creation and predictability. Following the chronological sequence of the seven days of the creation story, in tandem with Lectio Davina's reflections about these principles derived from Scripture, permitted trauma victims space to process and create art at their own pace and in their preferred way. This relieves people from emotional pressure. It also ensures an alchemy of creative artmaking in tandem with therapeutic psychotherapy that happens in a safe space. Without the feeling of safety and being accepted, no matter how wonderful the artmaking experience and reflection of the process might be, therapeutic processing should not be attempted. That is why a solid safe relationship with an accountable person is essential to the positive outcomes of the therapeutic process.

---

[227] Neuro-developmental art therapy (NDAT) consists of four phases of treatment over a long period of time and is designed to address relational trauma in children. It is directed at activating and developing the "lower structures of the brain, where relational trauma damage occurred," and it includes art and play activities. It seeks to integrate lower structures of the brain first in order to inform the higher functions later on, with the goal of moving the child to more improved capacities. Chapman's model does not assign a number of sessions to each phase but it is designed as a continuum with specific brain-related themes (neural activity, cognition, information processing, psychological reactions, and arts-based processes. L. Chapman on *Neurobiologically Informed Trauma Therapy with Children and Adolescents: Understanding Mechanisms of Change* (New York: Norton, 2014), 50. In Cathy A. Malchiodi, *Trauma and Expressive Arts Therapy. Brain, Body, & Imagination in the Healing Process* (New York: The Guilford Press, 2020), 71.

ART THERAPY VIEWED FROM
A BIBLICAL PERSPECTIVE

From what we know about the essence of art therapy and Levine's philosophical views, one can argue that the therapeutic modality—if skillfully applied—can assist in healing trauma wounding and injury. Furthermore, skillful implementation of these creative and imaginative artmaking therapeutic interventions allows insight into the processing of the person's psyche and hopefully assists in the healing process. However, I do not believe that artmaking alone, when used as a tool during therapeutic interventions, can be the ultimate key or cure to ending psychological suffering. God is the ultimate healer, not the instrument used in the process. Apart from the creative process at work, interventions must be prayerfully executed. When successfully implemented, these therapeutic directives can be viewed as tools that are utilized to assist in the manifestations of God's grace and Holy Spirit's intervention to lead the person toward new insights and wisdom on how to proceed with their lives after they have addressed an element of the trauma story. Therapeutic art interventions help to guide people's subconscious processes for reflection about and meaning-making of the trauma. In that way, integration happens. My yearning for holistic wellness for you reader to engage with creative artmaking and the GENESIS approach, is not inspired by humanism or the premise that creative artmaking alone has the power to bring complete emotional, mental, or spiritual healing and wellness. It is far more than that. God's love for his creatures and for you inspires this longing. The work of Holy Spirit during therapeutic artmaking interventions facilitates and assists in the healing process for the person to experience what Kapic describes as "a life lived to God".[228] When this happens, the Lectio Divina reflections and art-making process becomes sacred, magical, and mystical. This is in alignment with Victor Frankl's deep search for the meaning of life.[229] He believed that there are three main avenues to finding meaning in life.

---

[228] Kelly M. Kapic *A Little Book for New Theologians. Why and How to Study Theology.* (InterVarsity Press Downers Grove, Il, 2012), 42.
[229] Victor E. Frankl, *Man's Search for Meaning,* 5th ed. (Boston: Beacon Press, 1959),163.

The first is by creating a work or by doing a deed. The second is by experiencing something or encountering someone; in other words, meaning can be found not only in work but also in love. [T]he notion is that experiencing can be as valuable as achieving. It is therapeutic because it compensates for our one-sided emphasis on the external world of achievement at the expense of the internal world of experience. Most important is the third avenue to meaning in life: when even the helpless victim of a hopeless situation, facing a fate he cannot change, may rise above himself, may grow beyond himself, and by so doing, change himself. He may turn a personal tragedy into a triumph.[230]

CONCLUSION

Art therapy is about art itself, built on the premise that creative artmaking is at the centre of our humanity. Stephen Levine summarises it effectively when he says, "the act of *poiesis,* as "potential for creative existence, [which is found] in each one of us, can address human suffering"[231] when utilized during intentional safe psychotherapy. Artmaking has an inherent capacity to assist in the healing of the psyche. Art images can be beautiful, but in art therapy, though aesthetic, aesthetics is not the primary concern. Instead, it is about the creative process and the art techniques used to help free the imagination and the phenomena. Rubin explains that the "Theory underlying the approach is only meaningful and worthwhile if it helps to explain the phenomena with which it deals in a way that enables [the therapist] to do [her] work better."[232] Various art mediums are an indispensable component of the application of the

---

[230] Edith Weisskopf, The Place of Logotherapy in the World Today." *The International Forum for Logotherapy, Vol.1. No3. (1980) 3 -7.* In Victor E. Frankl, *Man's Search for Meaning,*5th ed. (Boston: Beacon Press, 1959),145.

[231] Stephen K. Levine, *Poiesis. The Language of Psychology and the Speech of the Soul* 2nd ed. (Palmerston Press, 1992), xvi.

[232] J. A. Rubin. Ed. *Approaches to Art Therapy. Theory and Technique* 3rd ed. (Routledge: Taylor and Francis Group, 2016), 5.

therapeutic process. Different media and artmaking techniques are essential because, when the therapeutic process is at play, art applications and techniques can be modified to adapt to the therapeutic process as it unfolds. That is also why the therapist must be well informed about other modalities to be used when needed in a hybrid relationship while the therapeutic artmaking continues. Art therapy must always occur in a safe environment, where therapists have respectful egalitarian relationships with their clients, with the notion that the individual has a say in the therapeutic process. Judith Rubin describes this as a reflection of a significant shift in the larger field of psychotherapy – from the therapist as the *expert* – "To a belief in the individual's ability to be not only in charge of his or her own life but also to be a partner in his or her therapy."[233] The therapist takes a stance of 'not knowing' and does not impose her belief system on the client. Furthermore, she should not assume to know what the art images represent, nor does she have prior knowledge about phenomena that can emerge from the person's imagination during therapeutic artmaking interventions.

Knowing that most art therapists believe that people are the experts of their own stories, the last chapters of this book, where the reader will process their trauma, also build on the premise that people know their life stories best. You the reader are the expert of your story. If you surrender to the guidance and assistance of Holy Spirit while engaging with the art directives, the embedded creativity deep within your soul can be unlocked. With the help of Holy Spirit, you will be able to co-create a new story, away from the chaos towards a New Beginning filled with hope and destiny.

[233] J. A. Rubin. Ed. *Approaches to Art Therapy. Theory and Technique* 3rd ed. (Routledge: Taylor and Francis Group, 2016), 4.

CHAPTER

CREATING FROM WITHIN

The conviction that Creator God desires all people to enjoy the pleasure of being creatively engaged in the world we live in, is embedded within my soul. Perhaps even more during times of pain and suffering. We know that creativity originated with God. God the Father created the world (Gen 1:1) through God the Son (Col.1:16; Heb.1:2). All creation was made through Him. Thus, He is the Creator God and the ultimate source of creativity. The ancient Greek philosophers explored creativity as a concept and introduced us to the process of *poiesis* which happens when we are creative. *Poiesis* [ποίησις] means "an activity in which a person brings something into being that did not exist before." This chapter is an invitation to, through the process of *poiesis* create art and reflect on inner experiences that caused you suffering. Added to the invitation is a request that you engage with the process in a prayerful stance, infused with a heart's desire to do it as a worshiper of the Living God. When pain and turmoil have invaded our lives, we must earnestly engage with a deeper sense of adoration and worship of the Trinity. This is not easy. That is why we often refer to praise as a sacrifice. Praise and worship become even more meaningful when they align with Scripture. The act of faithful obedience will enable you to move through, and away from the hurt and pain that have kept you in bondage. Creative praise and worship when manifested through artmaking is beautiful and glorious. Many trauma victims who surrender in adoration to the Lord, can testify how they discovered this way of processing to give them new insight and a pathway to life and hope again. Using art to help with your trauma healing management is an intensely personal process.

During intentional self-discovery and in-depth meaning-making of externalized art images and self-reflections about your pain story, you engage with processing of the trauma which helps you to discover new-in-depth meaning about your emotional wounding. Reflecting about the art image that you create allows for the trauma to show itself as a 'thingly thing." Allowing the trauma and its impact to emerge as an image that you can explore, is very helpful. Art therapists call this image, or 'thingly thing" that people create about the trauma experience, a *phenomenon,* which can be investigated in depth to help you understand what happened with you during the critical incident. Psychologist Stephen Levine, a trauma expert, says, "We need to let the phenomenon speak, help it to name itself, to tell its story."[234] So, when trauma emerges as a phenomenon or an image that you have created through artmaking, not only can it speak to you and tell you what you do not understand about your pain and suffering, but in turn it helps if you engage actively with the image that represents your trauma. This creative process and way of communication will help you to remember, and it also aids you to reframe and put the experience in a wider context. By doing that, you are enabled, and empowered, to re-member and re-story your painful encounters. This will provide you with an entirely different perspective.

PREPARATIONS FOR THE JOURNEY

This chapter is dedicated to preparing you for how to engage safely with trauma self-processing. Engaging with trauma processing requires deliberate action. Revisiting the dark trenches of trauma chaos also requires courage and can be likened to travelling into outer space. It demands preparation, determination and discipline. These steps and conditions must be explored and applied throughout the reading of this book if you desire trauma to be fully addressed and integrated

[234] Levine, Stephen K. *Trauma, Tragedy, Therapy. The Arts and Human Suffering* (London: Jessica Kingsley Publishers, 2009), 25.

as a cohesive life story. Intentional self-reflection means confronting the core of who you are. This is often very scary, but oh, so necessary. Avoiding addressing and challenging the issues that caused so much pain in the past will keep you trapped in darkness, where you will experience loneliness, fear, and anguish. Addressing and confronting your pain with self-compassion is essential. A crucial condition for effective self-care during self-reflection is to feel emotionally safe and stable before you engage with trauma processing. How does one stabilize your emotions? How do we create a safe space to launch into deeper emotional processing?

GROUNDING AND ANCHORING
MUST HAPPEN FIRST

Memory processing or trauma work can only begin when we feel safe and emotionally stable. It is important to ground and emotionally anchor yourself on something that you know to be true to you before you engage with a painful situation, or when you prepare to revisit painful memories. What can be safer than being in the presence of God? In Psalm 22:3 we read that God is enthroned in the praises of Israel. He is covenantal in this commitment, yes God's throne and authority are established in the praise of his children. This is the place He rules from. From his throne healing can flow to you after trauma has shattered your life. Praise and worship can start with your breathing. By deliberately focusing your mind on God and His character when you breathe intentionally, you already unlock an attitude of praise. Focusing on Emmanuel, God with us, you can invite Holy Spirit's guidance throughout the therapeutic process. You will need Holy Spirit to guide you. This is vital because when we process trauma at the cellular and spiritual level, we must engage with our spirit and we need His Spirit to do that effectively.

Another way to stabilize and regulate your emotions is to have enough oxygen in your brain. I suggest that you incorporate regular deep breathing exercises as a daily practice. You can do that by drawing your awareness to your breath. Breathe deep, strong, and slow breaths.

You can even take a sip of water before you do that. Breathe in and out... Relax your shoulders. As a reminder, these breaths are not meant for survival only, but they also have another special purpose, you need to breathe God's praises into the atmosphere. In your grounding, let your very breath continue to bring worship to God. Believers do not praise God only because they feel like it, but because He is worthy of it. Psalm 29:2 says, "Give unto the Lord the glory due to His name, worship the Lord in the beauty of holiness." Allow your awareness about who the Lord is, and aspects of his character to flow with the rhythm of your breath. Remain here for as long as needed. We read in Genesis 1 how the [rov'akh], which is the wind or breath of God's Spirit, was hovering over the face of the deep. Lingering over, and saturating the chaos, Holy Spirit spoke. In the same way, during seasons of chaos and the aftermath of trauma, you can allow Him to enter the mayhem and pain you are experiencing. By encountering what it is like to remain with Holy Spirit, you will experience the rhythm of divine lingering and the awakening of your own spirit, for His intervention to happen.

In addition, it is always helpful to develop the skill of mindful centring. How does one do that? By asking intentional questions in a contemplative way. Ask yourself, where am I? What is under my feet? What do I hear, what do I smell? Ah, what do I see? What is my skin touching? This sense of awareness will assist you to take hold of the present. Deliberate and mindful engagement with your senses means you become aware of what you feel and where you sense the feeling resides. Once you can acknowledge the feeling and where you can sense it in your body, allow this awareness to flow away gently. Imagine your awareness to be like a soft summer breeze moving over, and around you, without disturbing anything.

Starting on the journey towards emotional wounding processing, I invite you to embrace *loving-kindness* and *self-compassion*. When I use the word loving-kindness (*kheh-sed*), I think of it in the context where David reminded our Heavenly Father of his loving-kindness and tender mercies: "For they are from of old. Do not remember the sins of my youth, nor my transgressions; According to Your mercy remember me, for Your goodness sake, O Lord" (Psalm 25:6). Even if this is the first time for you to do so, use the example of the Lord's lovingkindness to mirror kindness and loving yourself, even if you think you do not deserve it. After all, it is not about deserving something, it is about grace and mercy, about giving freely. It is about following in the footsteps of Jesus. He gave his life and his love to you. If you can't love yourself, it becomes difficult to love others unconditionally. Judgment or self-criticism is the enemy of our souls. While working on your trauma story, and after that as well, remind yourself that you don't need a judge to evaluate or critique what you do. I want to reiterate that these moments of self-reflection must happen in a kind and self-accepting way.

This non-judgemental stance is particularly relevant when you begin working with creative artmaking reflections. It is easy to become distracted when you judge how you draw, or what you paint. When you create art, remember, it is always about the process, not the end product. Judging or criticizing yourself is a certain way to failure. There is no place for faultfinding or engaging with self-criticism. It has no role to play in your trauma recovery. Fire the critic! Remember, feeling safe, albeit just for these moments when you do reflective art, is essential. When we allow judgment or blame in our self-reflections, we cannot experience emotional safety. Rejecting your efforts when you try to do something for yourself, does not allow for stability or security.

Effective art journaling reflections work on a multi-dimensional level. It is not only about your thoughts but also about the feeling these images evoke when you reassess the trauma; By creating art your subconscious gets the opportunity to merge the memories, thoughts and feelings you carry about the trauma. All these elements of creativity are at a subliminal level necessary to process and make sense of *why* things happen to and with our lives. By touching, drawing, painting, or working with clay, wood, or other textures, those painful encounters you have stored in your subconsciousness are processed differently than worrying or mulling about them. This creative problem-solving approach can always be used again if you need to.

Another thing to be aware of, and to practice while you engage with trauma work, is to remember the importance of good sleep, enough water in your system, and yes, movement! Regular and consistent movement. Whether you choose to dance before the Lord, the way David or Miriam did, or naturally stroll down the street, don't underestimate the value of fresh air in your lungs while you move. It prepares your mind for processing the pain stories you are about to re-story. Following and executing these basic steps will prepare you for this pilgrimage through the valley and the shadows of your vulnerabilities. Get ready for, and expect that the artmaking and the reflections on the trauma processing will allow for tender moments, soft nuances and beautiful rhythms of creativity and self-discovery. Always be kind to yourself while doing that.

CURIOSITY IS YOUR FRIEND.

Allow for curiosity and inquiry about yourself, if possible, in a playful manner. To understand yourself well, you must be curious about who you are. What makes you tick? What do you love? Where do you find joy? What makes you happy? When you create your art, allow questions about the process. Wonder *why* you did what you did. Notice how you feel when you do what. All of these questions allow for self-discovery. Not only will you begin to be aware of who you are, but you will also notice who you are *becoming*. We are always in the process of growth; surrender to it. During these soul-searching moments, when you think about your process, you will discover more about your relationship with Holy Spirit, with the people in your life, and with your world. You will find out *who* played *what* role in your life.

While engaging in art making, we discover our priorities, which are essential in our lives. We learn anew why we have core values and what those are. We begin to understand that our core values impact and influence how we engage with one another. When you revisit your relationships with the people you love, you will begin to feel the stirrings and longings to make your relationships more meaningful. You will also realize which relationships must change, or to whom you can say goodbye to.

By engaging in a tactile way with art materials, you get in touch with the sensations in your body again. In this way, you can reconnect with your emotions and your feelings. As a result, your senses began to experience the world and God's beautiful creation anew. When used during self-reflection, creative art-making reflections and journaling help to tweak and re-story your life to become a stunning montage. This mosaic serves as a foundation to build on for the many more meaningful life encounters that await you.

YOU DON'T NEED TO BE A GOOD ARTIST

Being creative to process your pain story, does not necessarily mean you must be an artist to do so. In his Letter to Artists, Pope John Paul II states that we are not all called to be artists, but, as we see in Genesis, he says "All men and women are entrusted with crafting their own life: in a certain sense, they are to make it a work of art, a masterpiece."[235] That implies when we deliberately engage with artmaking reflections to address and process emotional wounding, the willingness to do so, the act in itself becomes creative, evidence of obedience, a step of faith, a work of art. Beautiful for the Master Artist to behold. The images you will create during your journaling reflections should not be aimed at becoming 'works of art.' Instead, play with the art supplies to experience *what it feels like* when you work with them and when you create images. Always remember the *process* before *the product.* Draw your attention and awareness to your own process and notice where your thoughts take you while doing that. Of course, sometimes your mind will take you nowhere, which is ok too. Your subconscious will do the work. So, relax and let the process lead the way. If you do this regularly, you will discover the benefits of your *creative processing.*

When you have completed these art-making reflections, the way our Creator God created this world, your reflections and journaling will not only tell a new story away from chaos and trauma, it will also help you to negotiate for, and manage new self-care principles that are unique to who you are.

---

[235] Christine Valters Paintner, *The Artist's Rule. A Twelve-week Journey. Nurturing your Creative Soul with Monastic Wisdom.* (www.sorinbooks.com, 2011), 16.

PRIORITIZE FOR PROCESSING TIME

Your life matters, and you are important to God. Therefore, you must become assertive about what you need so that you will buy the time for your self-care. Nobody else can do it for you. Without time to process the trauma wounds you have suffered; your brain will remain stuck in that space where the trauma has been imprinted. The reality is that your brain and body have stored memories, imprinted when the trauma was incurred. Engagement to address these imprints requires time, lovingkindness, self-compassion, and re-storying. Setting priority time to participate in creative art-making reflections will be an excellent creative encounter and a gift to you and your loved ones. You cannot afford not to give it to yourself. Please make this journey a priority. Set time apart for reflection, prayer, and meditation to pursue more profound meaning and self-discovery. Your life has a purpose and makes sense. The trauma in your past was not for nothing. Allow the Potter to shape who you are supposed to be and surrender to the furnace's flame.

ART JOURNAL AND ART SUPPLIES

To effectively use the material in this book, you will need a journal or sketchbook, a pen, and some art supplies you like to work with. The invitation to use any art medium you want or like to experiment with is open. The choice is wide. It can be colour pencils or paints and brushes. Some people prefer creating collages, working with paper cuttings, doing needlework, knitting, baking, gardening, working with clay, doing metalwork, or carving and burning wood. The list is endless. Use the media that speaks to you. Allow yourself space to explore with different art supplies. Soon, you will discover each medium that you work with has a different texture that often allows for different sensations to come to the fore when you process your story. Each art medium can trigger deeply-seated emotions that you have stuffed down into your psyche because of your trauma encounter. These need to come into the light so that you can make meaning of them.

FIND A QUIET SPACE TO WORK

Making time for art-making reflections is essential to the success of this journey to recovery. Life is busy. Most people have hectic lifestyles. This means that you must make time to slow down and be quiet. Remember Jesus? He often sought quiet spaces and locations to pray and meet with His Father. Taking time to be alone does not mean isolating yourself, far from it. Further, it will help if you create or negotiate for a designated place to sit back, relax, breathe deeply, and make art. Deep breaths of fresh air go to the inner parts of your lungs and expel stuffiness and dust. Oxygen helps your brain to process with clarity.

Research has shown over and over that meditation positively affects people's health. Finding and identifying a particular space to meditate and pray, while working on your art reflections to process emotional injuries, is part of effective self-care. Once you have identified the space, declare it sacred. It is because you have dedicated it to be the place where you have an appointment with Holy Spirit who will guide your reflections, meditations, and prayers.

Your quiet spot can be anywhere; next to the fireplace, under a tree in the garden, with the birds humming, or on a towel surrounded by soft sand on a seashore with the rhythmic waves of the ocean in the background. It can be on a chair next to the lake. For some, it will be on a bench in your community park, with children in the distance, playing soccer or sliding down a hill. For others, it can be the coziness of your bedroom or the study. For some, it will be in the kitchen at a clean countertop, after the busyness of preparing for school and work has slowed down and some calm has finally settled in.

FIND YOUR IDEAL QUIET TIME

Just as important as knowing where you will be when you reflect on your story, is what time of the day you are setting apart for it. Every person has their rhythm. For most, their ideal quiet time will be in the early morning, but for some of us, it will be much later in the evening when everyone else has gone to bed. Determine what time will be the best for you and prioritize it. When it is time to engage with self-care, go to your special place of solace, and be willing to linger there as long as needed. I suggest that you surrender this season in your life to the Lord. Dedicate it to Him and invite Holy Spirit to have full sway. Focus your hope and prayers on your healing and growth. Declare the season holy unto the Lord. Honour your declaration.

REFLECTIONS DIFFER

Your art-making reflection times will be different each time. Prepare yourself to be surprised. By surrendering this season of self-care to Holy Spirit, each of these interventions and reflections will become like an intimate dance. Submitting your story of pain and anguish to Holy Spirit, he can change even the most painful memories about those encounters. This can lead to a newfound revelation where you can find purpose again. Yes, trauma which previously felt unbearable, can be seen in a different light when it has been processed well. Addressing our pain in the light of God's love can lead us to encounter unfathomable dimensions of lovingkindness and mercy. Sometimes art-making reflections can leave a person feeling ignited with determination for transformation. This can help with prioritization and new energy to engage with change. It is a great confidence builder when you know you have received the right key to unlock a door you thought was locked. These different encounters can result in your acquiring the wisdom to know which door should remain closed for the season, and which one was staring you in the face, waiting for you to enter. A commitment to honouring these sacred quiet times where you are willing to process unresolved trauma that keeps you in bondage allows opportunities for enlargement where you can open your heart and discover wisdom that results in a life filled with passion, and purpose, with the necessary tools to move confidently into the future.

APPLY SELF-COMPASSION, BE REALISTIC AND PATIENT

Promoting meaningful reconstruction and meaning-making when trauma has challenged your assumptions about the world, is not easy. It is also tedious. When your hopes and dreams have been shattered, and your identity has been challenged, revisiting the memories and experiences around it is painful. However, a precondition for effective trauma processing requires that you choose change. It asks patience and compassion for yourself. Trauma processing is a journey, not a race. For trauma fragmentation and emotional wounding to be processed and assimilated in our lives, our goal is to re-tell the story of emotional pain in such a way that these fragmented memories and images can become a coherent self-narrative again. A new narrative, a different story that makes sense, must emerge. Doing that requires surrendering to a flow and process that will uniquely make sense for you, and nobody else. Every person experiences their trauma, in their own way. There is no perfect blueprint that will work the same way for everybody. You are unique, your story is yours. You are walking in your shoes that fit your feet. No one else can identify with what you are going through, no matter how hard they might try. Permit yourself to process in your own time, and in your unique way. Holy Spirit knows what you need and will walk alongside you as the Paraclete, or Helper when you do that. Surrendering this process to Him will help you to be patient and kind to yourself.

A TIME TO MOURN

King Solomon, the very wise king, said "To everything there is a season, a time for every purpose under heaven: ...a time to plant, And a time to pluck what is planted;... and a time to heal; A time to break down, and a time to build up; a time to weep, And a time to laugh; A time to mourn...(Eccl 3)." After suffering, and for healing and life integration of the pain, you must also learn how to mourn effectively. John Bowlby, an attachment theorist, explains that *people who fail to mourn loss might go on to feel deeply unsatisfied with their lives,* experiencing emptiness in personal relationships, depersonalization, and a sense of hopelessness for a very long time.[236] Some never recover. I hope that you will learn how to grieve, mourn and yes, lament, after trauma has invaded your life story

It is unrealistic to think you can address all the emotions and pain you have encountered in your lifetime by reading and working through a book only. Bear that in mind, and be willing to seek additional counselling if, and when you need it.

AN ACCOUNTABILITY PARTNER

People were created with connection in mind. You and I are meant to be in a relationship with others. We need people on our journey. This means you will need a witness to share your artmaking reflections about your pain story. We need witnesses on our life journey. Finding a friend that you trust enough to talk to while you work through the trauma story will make the reflections even more legitimate. When someone cheers you on it becomes easier to implement the changes you want to see happen. Where does one find an accountability partner? Do you know someone who cares about you and wants to see you happy and more fulfilled? Who is trustworthy and honourable and will not share your story with others? Who is willing to take some time to listen to you without judgement, or trying to give advice or interfere in your process and story? Who will encourage you? Who will commit to praying for you while you travel on this journey? Who will love your art images even though your art might differ from what they like? This person doesn't have to be artistic. Take some time to think about who you can ask to be your accountability partner. Then, ask that person if they are willing to commit to the process. Don't beat yourself up if you don't find the right person immediately. It might take some time to find the right fit. Remember, it is not a lifelong commitment, and you do not have to share your story's deepest secrets with that person if you don't want or

---

[236] Bowlby, J. (1982). Attachment and loss: Retrospect and prospect. *American Journal of Orthopsychiatry, 52*(4), 664–678. https://doi.org/10.1111/j.1939-0025.1982.tb01456.x

need to. It is a commitment to support you on this journey. They do not have to be a counsellor to do that. You are the one who will do the work, you are the one who will delve deep into your inner landscape to process your trauma. Your accountability partner only needs to cheer you on. If you can't find the right accountability partner, I encourage you to consider engaging with a local church community. Reach out to the pastor and ask if she or he will be willing to partner with you during your season of processing.

Once your accountability partner has agreed to walk with you for the duration of this season of healing, you are almost ready to begin the work. Now you only need to schedule your regular times for prayer, meditation and artmaking reflections. Keep to these times, make appointments with your accountability partner to report on your progress, keep to it, and continue to ask Holy Spirit to be your Helper.

CLEAN UP!

Closings are essential, also when you do art. When you finish your artmaking, please clean up when you are done. This is not only for practical reasons, but therapeutically it makes sense. After we have unpacked our emotional stuff, it is essential to create a space for calm and completion of a task to settle in. Cleaning the art space and utensils after deep processing and reflecting, will allow you some time between the moments of intense reflection to prepare for engagement with the world outside your private space. While cleaning and packing your art supplies, see it as an opportunity to integrate your emotions, stabilize your feelings and get more perspective. It helps you to normalize your emotions and prepare you for the demands of life outside of the therapeutic space.

DIFFERENT ART INTERVENTIONS

Some people do not like to work with one art medium or one way of art-making only. That is actually part of the playfulness that therapeutic art-making allows us. Just like there are no right or wrong ways to do art reflections, using colours and different textures, patterns or mediums is entirely up to what you prefer to do. For example, we know that people have preferences for certain colours and that these colours will often translate moods, feelings or emotions. The longer people work with different colours, the more their preferences will change. I will list a few common colour associations as compiled by Cathy Malchiodi below. However, remember that every person can prefer a certain colour for a specific reason and generalizations can be dangerous.

> **Blue:** sky, water, sea, heaven, spirituality, relaxation, cleansing, nourishing, calm, loyalty
>
> **Black:** darkness, emptiness, mystery, beginning, womb, unconsciousness, death, depression, loss
>
> **Brown:** fertility, soil, sorrow, roots, excrement, dirt, worthlessness, new beginnings
>
> **Green:** earth, fertility, vegetation, nature, growth, cycles of renewal, envy, overprotectiveness, creativity
>
> **Orange:** fire, harvest, warmth, energy, misfortune, alienation, assertiveness, power
>
> **Red:** birth, blood, fire, emotion, warmth, love, passion, wounds, anger, heat, life (danger)[237]
>
> **Violet/purple:** royalty, spirituality, wealth, authority, death, resurrection, imagination, attention, excitement, paranoia, persecution
>
> **White:** light, virginity, purity, moon, spirituality, creation, timelessness, dreamlike, generativity, resurrection, clarity, loss, synthesis, enlightenment

---

[237] Cathy A. Malchodi, ATR, LPCC/. *The Art Therapy Sourcebook,*(New York: McGraw. Hill 2007) 158.

SELF-CARE IS IMPORTANT

Finally, commitment to effective self-care is vital. Below is an example of a self-care agreement. It includes space for planning and strategies on how and when you will engage with the process. Revisit and then complete it in a way that will work for you. You can share your commitment agreement with your accountability partner to read, and even sign as a witness to this wonderful process. Doing that is an agreement to pray for, and encourage you on this road toward emotional healing.

CREATIVE SELF-CARE STATEMENT

Trauma invaded and damaged parts of my life. I want to reclaim the parts that were broken or stolen. I realize I have a role to play in restoring the story of my life. To do that I must engage with integrity, solely dependent on Holy Spirit to guide me. I am willing to address the issues that prevent me from full engagement with life, the way God desires for me to do. Like most other people, I suffered deep emotional pain and trauma that continues to hinder my maturity and growth. I no longer want these issues to hinder my growth. I therefore commit myself to engaging with effective self-care to address these issues and process them to the best of my ability. Here is the list of issues that I want to address by embarking on the GENESIS way to process my pain story:

_____

_____

_____

_____

_____

_____

_____

_____

_____

Name and signature _____

Date _____

PROCESSING YOUR TRAUMA
THE GENESIS WAY

Beginning with the process to address a pain story that has shaken the core of your existence negatively, is always daunting. I understand that too well. I know what it feels like when the pain and despair are so intense that it forces you on your knees, leaving you crying out to God for mercy. Oh, the searing pain that you experience when agony stirs your soul, and you think you have nowhere to go, and nobody can help. At those times painful memories can return to haunt and torment you. And worst of all, at those times it feels as if your willpower is not strong enough to push it away.

That is partly why this book was written, to help you make sense of the story of pain, and also to assist you in processing those trauma memories. When you do that, you will soon discover that prayerful meditations and making art to help you reflect on what is going on in the innermost parts of your being helps. Not only does it make your life bearable, but it is also enriching and life-giving. Research has shown that active engagement with creative artmaking is always therapeutic. Further to this, we have learned that deliberate art interventions make trauma processing not only safe but also enjoyable and have wonderful and positive outcomes.

Assisting you with processing your pain story, in the last chapters of the book, the interventions and directives you are introduced to are systematically organized and clinically thought through. The approach used is based on clinical research on how to address trauma. But it is also Scripturally sound. How does the process unfold? All art-making directives and interventions you are invited to participate in commence with a grounding reflection on the Scripture verses as introduced in Genesis 1. These directives and your engagement with Scripture adhere to basic Lectio Divina steps.[238] *Lectio Divina* are Latin words. They mean *Divine reading*. Historically it was seen as a monastery practice of scriptural reading, meditation, and prayer to make Scripture come

---

[238] *Lectio* (**Reading**): In the first phase of *lectio divina*, we understand what the passage we are reading says. This is the literal meaning of the Scripture passage and the lessons everyone should recognize in reading it... We do not let our opinions influence our reading but seek to understand the passage's message as interpreted by the Church independently of anyone's opinions. This phase is summarized with the question: *What does the text say everyone should understand?*

Meditatio (**Meditation**): In the meditation phase of *lectio divina*, we ask, *what does this text say to me, today, and my life?* We allow God to pull up certain memories of people, places, and events in our lives that relate to the passage we read. Meditation is also an opportunity to see ourselves in the text. We can consider our own feelings as if we were a participant in the text or try to understand what it would be like to be one of the people represented in the text. In this way, we come to a deeper appreciation of how God is working in our lives through the sacred word. Having entered into the story ourselves, we can return to the present and consider the areas in our lives that God calls us to contemplate.

Oratio (**Prayer**): Through a meditation on Scripture, we experience an intimate encounter with God that leads us to respond in prayer. Having met our Lord in his holy word, we courageously speak to him in our own words. In this way, we consider prayer to be a simple conversation with God. It is a conversation that comes in various forms: we ask him petitions (or requests), and give him thanks, and praise. At this phase, we can ask ourselves: *What can I say to the Lord in response to his word?*

Contemplatio (**Contemplation**): A true encounter with the Lord always leads to transformation. Indeed, the Lord God proclaimed, "Behold, I make all things new" (Revelation 21:5). Through contemplation, we come to an understanding of the parts of our lives that need to be transformed by God's grace. We humble ourselves and open our lives up to his transformative power. This step comes with the willingness to change, openness and trust in God, and the decision to follow God's will rather than our own. With this decision comes a fear of losing what we find comfortable and safe. At the same time, we feel the excitement of a call to heroic adventure and a hopeful future of living the life we are meant to live. At this step in the *lectio divina* process, we ask ourselves: *What conversion of the mind, heart, and life is the Lord asking of me?*

Actio (**Action**): Finally, although this phase is often not considered to be a part of *lectio divina* proper, it is an essential result of the encounter with God in Sacred Scripture. "We do well also to remember that the process of *lectio divina* is not concluded until it arrives at action (*actio*), which moves the believer to make his or her life a gift for others in charity" (no. 87). Having received God's love and grace, we go forth to serve others out of the love we have been given. Our transformation calls us to witness to others; it calls us to serve our brothers and sisters in Christ selflessly. These acts are done not so much out of a sense of duty, but out of the inspiration we receive from the acceptance in faith of God's love., Pope Benedict XVI in the post-synodal Apostolic Exhortation, *Verbum Domini* (nos. 86-87), accessed on February 2, 2023. https://www.vatican.va/content/benedict-xvi/en/apost_exhortations/documents/hf_ben-xvi_exh_20100930_verbum-domini.html

alive to monks who used it to meditate on the Bible. Most people who are serious about the Bible, prefer to engage with Scripture the *Lectio Divina* way. Today we understand and enjoy the benefits of this approach to meditate on Scripture. These steps to engage with the Bible are simple and easy to follow. Lectio Divina's reflections always start by reading Scripture reverently and prayerfully.

It is best to read Scripture verses in its context. While reading, try to find some portions of the text that stand out to you. Take hold of it. If necessary, write it down. Attempt to memorize it, or at least some of the words or concepts which stand out to you.

Meditate on it. As a child, growing up on a farm, I was mesmerized by the way the cows chewed their cud. We now know dairy cows spend almost eight hours daily chewing on their cud. That is about 30,000 chews per day! Meditation at its core correlates with how a cow eats grass which eventually becomes milk. The cow chews, re-chews and then chews again until the grass finally turns into milk. Meditation takes time. It is a slow process of gradual unfolding. During meditation on the Scripture, images, memories, and the feelings related to those memories in the context of the Bible verses might begin to stir deep inside your inner core. Mindful engagement with your senses while reading Scripture is helpful. Knowing what your body feels when you read certain parts of Scripture makes these meditations even more real and experiential. When you contemplate these Bible verses, and if an image relating to your meditation comes to mind, try to engage with your body when it happens. See if you can sense some sensation in your body.

Not all people see pictures or images when they read. Some people, mostly left-brainers, have difficulty to 'see' an image in their mind. That is ok, you don't have to work on trying to get an image if it is not happening for you. Some people have a feeling or a sense of awareness in their bodies when they meditate on Scripture. When that happens, try to get a sense of your body, where you feel it, and how it feels when you read the portion. If you get this kind of awareness, identify it, then, slowly breathe through those feelings and gently allow them to flow away.

Pray. When a particular concept from the Scripture begins to stir within you, tune into it, pray about it again, and speak to God about it. Remember, prayer is a conversation with the Lord. Allow Holy

Spirit to direct your conversation. Listen intentionally to what you are praying. These conversations will provide you with some helpful clues, and often directives as to where Holy Spirit wants to take you in your contemplative journey with Him.

Contemplate. Remember, contemplation is a slow process. Be patient with yourself. Think, consider, and re-consider the thoughts and images that came to your mind while praying. Self-observation allows for transformation and change. Reflect on these things that came up for you while you were in meditation and prayer. Consider what you have come to understand and think about. And then, take it even a step further by thinking about what actions you could take that might be necessary to engage with because of these new insights that came to your mind.

Action. All true transformation happens with one action first. *Choice*. Only humans can execute free choice. To choose includes the capacity and ability of decision-making. When that happens one can expect that change is possible. To be able to choose is mysterious and simultaneously wonderful. Determine what kind of change you want to see in your life. Name it, and then execute your God-given gift of choice to choose for that change to happen. Embracing your gift of choice helps you to make decisions and assertively implement them. Once the decision has been made, you will discover the conviction and confidence to follow through and complete the journey towards trauma recovery.

While engaging with Lectio Divina principles and steps, the invitation is to participate in artmaking with an open mind and heart. Do it in a playful stance, like a little child who plays, without judgment or self-condemnation. Do it with abandonment and full engagement. I want to remind you of the lovely concept of *poiesis* that takes place when you make art. Even your initial attempts and experimentation with the different art mediums can bring about a self-awareness about your way of being in the world. When you "occupy" the artmaking experience, an indwelling of your creative self, and insight about your subconscious process occurs. Turning inward with intent and attention to immerse yourself in some facet of the creative experience, you will gradually discover profound insights about your psyche and the emotional layers that can rise to your awareness. But that is not all, after the image has been completed and even while you are busy cleaning up, you will become aware of a shift in your awareness about the trauma story you have revisited while working on the art.

When you reflect on the art images, new illuminations about yourself or situations in the past often come to the surface. These enlightenments happen when hidden meanings, distortions or areas that need correction in how you engage with the trauma story can be perceived. A unique insight into some trauma triggers related to forgotten memories or painful experiences can also emerge at this time. Prepare your heart for these insights, write them down, and if necessary, discuss them with your accountability partner. In that way, new meaning-making about the incident can begin to emerge.

Once you have gained insight and light about the situation or the trauma event, the re-storying processes can begin. These new perspectives gained about the reflections from Scripture can be applied to you because they are personal and relevant to your life. Amazingly, you will find that once these insights are logically processed, they can be integrated and a new narrative about the traumatic experience will start to form in your mind. It somehow becomes possible to talk more easily about the incident, and what you have learned from it. Therapists call it creative synthesis when all, or most of the questions around a person's emotional wounding have been processed, answered, and integrated.

People need closure to move forward and onward with their lives. The art images you have created during your processing will assist you in providing a beginning, a middle and an end to the trauma event and the experience. It is as if a circle has come to completion. We call that closure. The painful story has a beginning, you have re-storied the middle, and the end has a period. Once that has played out, you will experience that trauma does have an end and that it is indeed possible to move forward, and away from the past. When that happens, your pain has been successfully integrated into your life mosaic, and you can move towards living a life that does not keep you imprisoned in the past anymore. In the next chapter, you will find the practical application where you will process your soul wounding through therapeutic art-making reflections with the help of art directives that were designed with principles derived from the Creation Story and how God created beauty out of ashes and chaos.

CHAPTER

GENESIS - DAY ONE

The Journey Towards Integration and Emotional Healing

The earth was without form, and void; and darkness was on the face of the deep. And the Spirit of God was hovering over the face of the waters. Then God said, "Let there be light; and there was light. And God saw the light, that it was good; and God divided the light from the darkness. God called the light Day, and the darkness He called Night. So the evening and the morning were the first day" (Genesis 1:1-5).

In the very first verse of the Bible, we read that God was present when the world we know and love was created. Not only was the Lord present, but He also created it! Every single detail of this awesome creation was His doing. In Genesis 1, we are introduced to God as Elohim, the divine, eternal, and ever-present God. The God who is the Everlasting one, the One who was, who is, and who will always be, is also Creator God. The great I Am who knows you by name, is the author and finisher of this wonderful story of creation. He is also the One who can intervene and create anew in your life. Trauma victims whose lives have plummeted into chaos need to embrace the reality that God's creative ability did not cease after He created the world. This is important. How do we know that? Let us look at the story of Abraham in Genesis 17 verse one onwards. Abram was childless and already ninety-nine years old when

God spoke to him about his future. He introduced himself and said, "I am the Almighty God (El Shaddai) who, if I don't have something, I will create it…" This is mind-blowing! Creator God can create something from nothing. All the time. God has not changed. When it feels as if trauma has derailed your life, and everything has imploded around you, this is not the end, our Creator God can create an entirely new and beautiful story away from the ashes and pain that you have suffered.

This is indeed good news for a person who suffered trauma and who has lost all sense of safety and security. To move towards restoration, the trauma victim must regain some sense of protection, security, safety, and predictability. The first step in trauma treatment is therefore always aimed at addressing insecurity, uncertainty, and instability. This will be the step you will work on during your first *lectio divina* reflection. During the reflection and the artmaking activity, you will reflect on the omnipresence and eternal reality of God who never changes, who can create anew, and who loves you. At the beginning of this journey towards processing your trauma and pain, I invite you to be reminiscent of the Creator God who not only was at the beginning of all things, but He was also present *at your own beginning.* Yes, the ever-present God was there. Nothing was hidden from him. Even at your conception, Creator God of the universe was actively involved with you in mind. In the sacred space of your mother's womb, in that silent circle where there was utter darkness, your Creator who spoke light into existence, also said "Yes" for you to become human. He breathed his life-giving Spirit into you and propelled you to become a person with a soul and his spirit to indwell you. Holy Spirit connected with you. Your body became spirit-indwelled.

For nine months He weaved you together, moulded you, and grew you. When He formed your inward parts, you were safely protected. The psalmist says you were fearfully and wonderfully made, skillfully put together. He created you as unique, deeply loved, and wonderful. Yes, there is no other person exactly like you. And, remarkably, His Spirit is still with you and hovering over you! His ability to create anew has not ended. In everything you do and experience, He knows you. Even when your days are gray and if your life feels miserable, He has never lost sight of you. The Lord knows how much hair is on your head!

That He has numbered each hair on my head leaves me speechless. I was reminded of this when I lost all my hair during cancer treatment. During seasons of pain and despair, our God who spoke the world into existence, also knows the emotional, physical, and mental pain that you have experienced in your life. He is aware of the chaos that followed. And then comes this wonderful assurance, your Creator remains interested in you. His care and concern have never wavered. His love for you endures.

So many trauma victims, believers who have surrendered their lives to God, and followed Him in the best way they could, have said, "Yes, I know God loves me, but it certainly does not feel that way." They then ask: "How and where do I begin to anchor myself when everything around me feels unstable, and I have no hope or energy left for things to change? What do I do after trauma has stripped away everything that has meant something to me when the core of my existence feels under threat of disintegrating?" The answer is not simple, but I am convinced the time when we feel the least like embracing it when our despair is at its peak, is the time to dig in our heels and remind ourselves of the reality of the Creator of the universe, who is the Almighty and the Ever-present God. He has not changed, and He never will. He is still able to create anew. He knows the narrative of your entire life. The Great Potter can pick up every shattered piece of your life, remould it, and create a beautiful masterpiece. He did it in times past and still does it today. Our God is good, and He has your best interest at heart. His desire for you is to lead a grace-filled life in His abundance. An everlasting life. A life in companionship with Him. In the same way, He desired Adam and Eve to have a relationship with Him in the Garden of Eden. We must revisit this universal truth often during painful seasons in our lives.

Some reflection about the Garden of Eden. In the book of Genesis 2:8 onward, we read about a mysterious and lovely place, a garden of delight, beauty, and luxury where God enjoyed fellowship and communion with Adam and Eve, the first people He created. Adam and Eve roamed freely in and around the beauty and abundance of Eden. Apart from tending to the garden and its lush produce, Adam not only had the joy of observing every living creature that God created, but when

God was finished, He would present the creature to Adam, who was invited to decide on and provide each one with a name befitting them! Every creative action of God was like the creation of a new song, where melody, harmony and rhythm came together, and Adam provided the lyrics. God, the Creator of the universe would dream about and then create a work of art, whereafter Adam had the opportunity to observe, identify and then speak forth about God's handiwork. But this did not last. We learn that due to Satan's cunning manipulation, and Eve and Adam's subsequent rebellion against God, humankind lost the privilege of intimate fellowship with God. They lost all that splendour and joy because of their sin. What a tragedy! But the story does not end there. God's desire for fellowship with humanity has not stopped. The Good News is that because of Jesus Christ, who died for our sins, believers can be grafted into the Tree of Life, and we can enjoy that fellowship as it was in Eden with our Heavenly Father once more. Yes, even after trauma, you can know and embrace the beauty of His restoration power, and His healing love all over again. Our Lord is the God of New Beginnings. Creator God wants you to experience and enjoy joy, peace and righteousness, here and now. This is not only possible but also your gift. He made provision for this more than 2000 years ago when Jesus died on the cross. Jesus, the Christ conquered sin and death and rose again. This is wonderful, glorious Good News. So, come along, let's begin with the journey toward sense-making and integration of the painful chaos that you are experiencing right now.

Invitation

As a reminder about clinical research related to trauma treatment, we know one of the foundational conditions for effective trauma processing is that a person must feel safe and emotionally stable before they can address any emotional pain. I want to make sure that you experience that safety before you engage with any trauma work.

- Begin by *pausing, grounding* and *anchoring* yourself in the character and steadfastness of God.

- Commence with intentional breathing. Intentional breathing implies that you deliberately focus your mind on how you breathe.
- As you remind yourself about our Heavenly Father as the Creator, think about the beginning of the creation in Genesis.
- While deeply inhaling, and slowly exhaling, contemplate and ground yourself solidly around the fundamental principle that *God never changes.*
- Anchor your thoughts around Elohim, the eternal Creator. Stay with this grounding character trade of God. Do it until you feel your mind is fixed around the concept of Creator God, who was there in the Beginning, and who is still here...

Once you can do that, and with these deep and slow breaths as the foundation, I invite you to pray with me:

Grounding Prayer

"Thank you, Heavenly Father, Creator of all, that You were present at the beginning of all things, also when Earth was created. Holy Spirit, you were there as well. Jesus, you are the Word who was in the beginning, and the Word who was with God. All things were made through you, and without you, nothing was made that was made. In you was life, and the life was the light of men. And the light shines in the darkness, and the darkness does not comprehend it. Heavenly Father, You were with me at the beginning of my own life when I was conceived, and You are still here with me now. Jesus, you are the Word who has called me by name when Father God had me in mind at the beginning of my creation. I am yours. You are in me, and I am grafted into you. Thank you, Lord, that, during this time when I desire to work on my own pain story, you will remain present. Holy Spirit thank you for knowing how to hover and remain, even in the darkest nights. I praise and worship you for your grace and ever-abiding love. Amen."

Artmaking activity

The following activity is intended for you to experience predictability, continuation, and what we imagine endlessness feels like. You will do that by creating and working within a circle. We know that a circle has no beginning and no end.

- First, you will practice circle formation by making a circle in the air with your arms. You can use one, or both arms to do that. This activity can be done while you are sitting, or if you want to, you can stand up to do it. Draw circles with one arm or both in the air before you. While doing that, try to close your eyes and think about the omnipresence of God.
- Meditate about the eternal Creator. The ever-present God who was present at the beginning of all things. Father God was also there when you became a human being, a person, created in His image. He encircled you…
- Try to visualize what it looks like to be safely surrounded by love.
- Feel what it feels like to be inside this circle of protection. Go with the rhythm of the movement of your arms until you think it is enough.
- Slowly breathe in and out. Savour this sense of encircled sheltered-ness.
- When you are ready, proceed to your art materials and your art journal. Open it up and draw a circle. This circle can be any size, providing that it fits on the canvas or your journal before you.
- Begin to create art within this circle. The intention is to create art while you think about God as the *stable Life Force that will never leave or forsake you*. While working on your art, think about this concept of God.
- Remember, there are no rules on how you should create. You can draw or paint anything when you work on a reflection. You can draw an image, or shapes and patterns. You can add colours, change mediums, and do what you like. I want you to be playful while you do this.

- Stay within this complete circle as long as needed. Remind yourself that the circle has no beginning or end.
- If you are ready and want to, you can move outside the circle and continue your artmaking there.

Observation

While working on your art, your mind might take you to thoughts about God as actively aware and present at your beginning. But that is not always the case. The act of engaging with the art material has its way of leading you through a process. It can take you to thoughts or memories you have never thought of. That is ok. Experiment, play. Remember to enjoy the art-making without too much thought about the result. Savour these creative moments in the flow and spirit of how it could have been for God when He was creating you. Try to participate in the feeling and the rhythm of the creative process. Do not rush yourself. Stay with the process as long as you need to.

- Once you are done with the image, put your art supplies down. Now is your opportunity to step back, away from being with the circle, to be with the art. You have done your work. The canvas has the story. You are now ready to allow some distance between you and the image. Place your canvas or art journal in a spot where you have a good look at it to see what you have done. This helps to put your process in perspective.

Reflection

Congratulations, you have engaged with your first therapeutic art activity on this journey to address the pain story that has haunted you for a long time. By working in a circle, you have created a safe place where God is present with you, to work from and to build on. Permit yourself to silently, and without judgment, revisit the image that you have made. Look intently, as if you are seeing it for the first time. Observe your emotions and thoughts, but don't try to analyze or hold onto them too tightly, breathe over them and let them flow away.

Contemplation

Ask yourself:

- How did it feel to work within a circle?
- What thoughts about God's steadfast love, omnipotence, creativity and involvement in my life come to mind when I see the image in the circle?
- How do I feel when I see this image? What do I see?
- What thoughts come to mind when you see it?
- What colours did you use?
- Did the colours you used have a specific meaning to you? What did it mean?
- Was there a combination of colours in the circle? Did you repeat it?
- Do you like the image? Why or why not?
- Is there something that you like about the image that you have created? What is it?
- Are there things that you dislike?
- Are there things in the image that you wish were different?
- Are there shapes or patterns in the image that repeat itself? What are they?
- Are you observing some interesting things about the image that you wonder about?
- Look again, and ask, what else do I also see? Is there something missing? Do I want to change something? If so, change or add it.

Journaling

Take some time to write about your thoughts and feelings. Reflect on your awareness and possible questions you might have related to your art image. Allow time to reflect and write about your self-awareness, and what you have learned about yourself, God or others while working in the circle. Allow yourself to think about the reality that Creator God was present with you at your beginning. This is a wonderful concept and awareness. Allow this truth to sink in. If you want to write a poem or feel you want to sing a song about this beautiful beginning, now is the time to do so.

In closing, this creative activity was the beginning of a new process. You have successfully created art and initiated your first therapeutic art reflection around the grounding principle of God's unchanging and steadfast character, as signified by the circle. You have determined that Creator God, who was at the beginning in Genesis, is also your Heavenly Father who has created you. You have reaffirmed that He knows you intimately and personally. God's steadfastness is foundational to the entire process during the rest of the work you will do. It will anchor you for the duration of the healing journey. The principle of being grounded and centred on the complete steadfastness of God's character is the basis before any other therapeutic work should commence. Anchoring yourself in the character of God assists toward emotional self-regulation when you experience overwhelming feelings and flooding emotions. Staying grounded and anchored in the safety of God's steadfast love is a foundational condition for effective trauma processing to continue. This knowledge will carry you through when you revisit the traumatic encounters.

Once done with the art reflection, you can clean the work surface and pack away your art supplies. Tomorrow is another day. During the next artmaking reflection, you will get the opportunity to name the darkness. Darkness will become a metaphor for the story of pain and chaos that you have been experiencing because of trauma. But remember, you will not visit that darkness from a place of despair. This first intervention taught you how to anchor yourself in God's presence, encircled by his love and the awareness that Father God will be there with you, even in the darkest night of your soul.

Grounding Skill Development

Grounded-ness, or feeling protected and secure, is the first step toward emotional self-regulation. Self-regulation happens when people can manage and control their emotions instead of allowing their feelings to take over. When your feelings take over and you feel out of control, it is called emotional flooding. Being able to modulate and regulate your feelings assists in making emotional wounding integration easier. A word of caution, the same principle needed for physical fitness applies to emotional health. It is something one must learn to do, and then consistently repeat. Remember, emotional self-regulation is very seldom possible at a first attempt. When a baby is upset or afraid, their first instinct is to cry. Likewise, after trauma, a person's emotions are raw and tender. Be patient and award yourself some time to practice self-regulation. Following is an activity that can help you safely develop and practice emotional self-regulation skills.

Emotional Regulation Skill-building

When memories become too painful your body and your emotions will react accordingly. It is helpful to know how to regulate your emotions when that happens. Here is a way to help when you feel emotionally overwhelmed:

- Stop what you are doing.
- Take a sip of water.
- Engage with intentional slow and controlled deep breathing while you send your thoughts to anchor around the principle of the safety of God's steadfastness.
- Permit yourself to offer a sacrifice of praise to the Lord for His constant love.
- Remind yourself of the circle of safety you have created through your art.
- Close your eyes while thanking the Lord for the security His presence brings. Doing this, allows for a moment of beauty and silence, even in the heat of an overwhelming flood of emotions.

Desensitization Skill-building

- Find a medium size dark blanket, thick towel or black toque.
- Hold the blanket on both sides and pull it over your head.

- Without moving, try to sit still and imagine what it feels like to be in total darkness without the ability to see anything. (Going into a dark closet could result in the same effect.)
- While you are sitting under the blanket, breathe deeply and slowly. Draw your attention to the sensations in your body. What do you feel? Where do you sense the feeling in your body?
- While you control your breathing, steer your thoughts to a negative experience in your not-too-far past. Check in with yourself, is there a change in your body when you think about this negative event? If so, what is it and where do you feel the change?
- Attempt to sit with this feeling while you control your breathing.
- Once you are certain you are managing your breath, relax and breathe normally. Do not rush it. If you can capture and hold the feeling without changing the rhythm of your breath, you are successfully regulating this feeling or emotion. You can now pull the blanket off and open your eyes.

GENESIS DAY ONE - MEDITATION TWO

Light versus Darkness

...and God divided the light from the darkness.
God called the light Day, and the darkness He called
Night. So the evening and the morning were the first day"
(Genesis 1:1-5).

The Wasteland of Trauma

People who are suffering because of trauma find themselves perpetually in a state of emotional chaos and turmoil. The traumatic event has shaken them to the core, and they feel abandoned, alone and in darkness. They are in a never-ending wasteland of misery. Ignoring these feelings of despair and chaos does not make it go away, let alone getting better. To be in such a dark place leaves people feeling helpless. Finding direction for life, making decisions, or even setting a goal, feels challenging. When we read about darkness and chaos in Genesis, it is described as *Tôhûw* or *Tôhûwaboho*. This Hebrew word originated from an unused root that means *"to lie waste; for example, to be in a desert; to feel like a worthless thing; when it is used as an adverb it means everything is in vain. That there is confusion, emptiness, formlessness, or nothing-ness, everything will come to nought or is vain. Everything is vanity or wasted. As if you are in a wilderness."*[239] This image of darkness and chaos can be seen or experienced as misery. *Tôhûwaboho* therefore explains the after-effects of trauma very well.

Because God was at the beginning where there was darkness and a wasteland, He also knows and understands your darkness. Not only did the Lord encounter darkness, but he addressed it head-on. After He separated the darkness and the chaos from the light, He then called

---

[239] Strong, James, *Strong's Exhaustive Concordance* (Hendrickson Publishers, 2009),123.

forth a new day. He wants to do the same for you. The Lord desires that you experience a new day away from the chaos and pain you have encountered for such a long time.

Breathe, pray, and meditate

In Genesis, coming into the light was described as an act of *illumination*. Try to visualize what it must have looked and felt like when Creator God first separated the light from the darkness. *"God divided the light from the darkness. God called the light Day, and the darkness He called Night. So the evening and the morning were the first day."* Illumination as a concept makes sense in the context of shining light onto a subject. Bringing enlightenment to a situation means you are assisted in finding clarity about something. When sunlight breaks through the darkness, misery can be dispelled. Holy Spirit can help you to feel safe and secure as well.

For this directive, you are invited to focus on the Creator God who distinguished and separated light from the darkness. If trauma resulted in a 'dark night of the soul for you, know this, your Creator can end darkness' reach in your life and limit its duration. By discerning the darkness, by naming it and surrendering it to him, you can trust the Lord to lead you into the light. When his light shines in, the darkness must flee. Daybreak has come.

Invitation

Hidden trauma kept secret, continues to haunt its prey. Today you will invite Holy Spirit to help you separate yourself from the darkness of the trauma you have experienced. Without identifying and naming your emotional pain, the effects of trauma remain secretive, unsaid and vague. Speaking up about its effects is vital for healing to begin. It is important to call out and name the damage that you have suffered. In that way, you can address it. Being an emotional wounding, addressing trauma must be done gently and with caution. If a person has been in a dark space for a prolonged period, a sudden bright light can blind that person if they suddenly look at the sun. - A temperate and peaceful separation process between light and darkness is healthy. Today, when you engage with artmaking, be patient with yourself, your feelings and the process. Allow for a gradual unfolding of the light to shine.

Art-making Directive

This art-making activity intends to *identify*, *name* and *externalize* the darkness and pain of the trauma you have experienced, in contrast to the joy of living a life filled with joy, peace and contentment. The art-making will be done within the confinement of a border. Before starting with your art reflection, read the instructions and close your eyes a while to let the instructions sink in. Do not rush it. Invite Holy Spirit to guide your art-making. Ask for clarity of mind.

- Make sure that you are seated in a comfortable position. You want to feel the earth underneath you.
- Divide the page into two sections. Use a pencil or oil pastel, any colour you like, and draw a border around the edges of your canvas or the art journal. The border can be as solid or thick as you want it. If the one page is too small for two images, you can work on two different pages.
- With your non-dominant hand, and within the first section of the bordered page, create art about the pain around and about the traumatic event which has caused you to feel trapped in chaos and darkness. This image can be anything or any shape but must express what the darkness in your life story looks and feels like. When you are done with the image, you can draw your attention to the other section or page.
- In this section, with your dominant hand, draw an image or shapes or patterns of the things you are grateful for, and what has the potential to fill you with joy.
- Do not rush yourself, remain with the artmaking as long as needed.

- Be mindful of your body. Try to remain aware of the physical sensations you could feel in your body while you work on your image. Notice these sensations and let them go.
- Once done with the art-making, step back and move away from the image.

Contemplation, Self-reflection and Journaling

Permit yourself to look in silence and without judgment at the art image you have created about your trauma story.

- What do you see? What do you think?
- Is there anything, maybe something small that you like? What is it?
- Is there anything you would like to change about this side? Why?
- Which emotions come to mind when you look at the darkness? What colours did you use?
- Are there any sensations in your body that you become aware of when you look at the darkness?
- Where do you feel it? What comes to mind when you linger at that place in your body?
- If possible, place your hand on the spot where you feel the sensation. It can be a feeling of warmth or something without words describing it. That is ok.
- Place your other hand on your heart or your stomach. Take a few moments to breathe deeply to release any anxiety or discomfort that you might experience. Allow the feeling to flow away when you slowly breathe out. Do this a few times until you no longer feel that sensation. Relax and come back to the complete artwork.
- Draw your focus to the image of light and joy. What do you think?
- What is at the centre of this image?
- Which colours did you use? Is there a specific colour, pattern or shape that stands out for you?
- How did you decide what elements to include?

- Are there any elements that you wanted to include but did not?
- Is there something you want to change? Go ahead and change it.
- If you could give a name or a title to the completed artwork, what would it be?
- Write down any thoughts and feelings, awareness or questions that might come to the fore as they relate to the story of pain and chaos as depicted in this image.
- What do you feel when you think about the fact that the darkness has a border? Would you have liked it if the border was thinner or thicker? Do you want the border to disappear? If so, why, or why not? Does the boundary around the darkness make you feel safer?
- Write down anything you have learned about yourself, the experience, and what the image revealed to you.
- Write three things you are grateful for because of this reflection.
- Surrender this gratitude as a prayer sacrifice to the Lord.

In closing

God Himself has set a limit on darkness. In Psalm 139 we read that even the darkness is as light to Him. Darkness can't continue, the light will always overcome. Once you have completed your reflection, you can relax and celebrate while cleaning your workspace. You have externalized a version of the pain that has haunted you for such a long time. This took courage. You were brave and set a limit to the pain story's reach. It is no longer hidden. You should not be surprised to feel exhausted after deep emotional processing like this. Make time and go for a walk, drink water and listen to music that soothes your spirit.

GENESIS, DAY TWO

The Space in Between and the Believer's Eternal Axis Mundi

Then God said, "Let there be a firmament amid the waters, and let it divide the waters from the waters." Thus God made the firmament and divided the waters which were under the firmament from the waters which were above the firmament, and it was so. And God called the firmament Heaven. So the evening and the morning were the second day

(Genesis 1: 6-8)

Meditation

Trauma destabilizes people. – It 'quivers our rhythm' so to speak. Like a tsunami, one critical incident can push us totally out of balance. In the believer's darkest hour, when it feels as if the entire universe has collapsed and heaven and earth become blurred, we do not know where we begin and where our sorrow ends. But then we can be reminded of Christ and what He has done for us. Just like the world's *Axis Mundi*, the line that stems through the earth's centre, and connects its surface to the underworld and the heavens, and around which the whole universe revolves, Christian believers each have an eternal *axis mundi* around which we circle and exist, and His name is Jesus, the Christ. He manifested in the liminal space of our existence and is the difference between the old you and the New Creation. He filled the vacuum between heaven and earth. He made the difference between death and life. Paul said: "In Him, we live and move and have our being... for we are also His offspring" (Acts 17:28 NKJ).

After trauma, getting our lives into perspective, we must, like the earth, 'tilt our axe towards the sun.' By anchoring our internal locus of control entirely on the character of God, we can stop the quivering of our souls. Our gaze should be solidly fixed on Him. We read, "Thou will keep him in perfect peace whose mind is stayed on Thee, because he trusts in You" (Isaiah 26:3). By choosing to trust in God's unfailing love you will experience what it feels like to be re-anchored after a season of sorrow and suffering. To recover from trauma our focus must be realigned with Truth. Re-establishing your attention on your *Axis Mundi,* as it pivots around Jesus Christ, will assist you in stabilizing and refocusing on what counts. With eyes and minds fixed on Christ, realignment can happen, and we can reclaim our memories and identity.

In Numbers 21:6-9, we read how many Israelites, while travelling through the Negev wilderness on their way to the promised land, were bitten by poisonous snakes and subsequently died. Traumatized and helpless to do anything to change their fate, they were all destined to die. Without a miraculous intervention from God, they had no hope for survival. But then, after consulting with God, Moses instructed Aaron to make a copper snake, then decreed for it to be lifted on a pole towards the heavens. When bitten by the snakes, the people who looked up to the copper serpent were healed and restored. This story was a foreshadowing of what was to come thousands of years later when Jesus was nailed and died on the cursed cross on our behalf. The Father's love for humanity, the sacrifice Christ made with his death on the cross, makes it possible for all who have suffered because of sin, unrighteousness, or trauma, caused by us or others, to be delivered. Every repentant sinner who looks to Him and accepts the price that Jesus Christ has paid with his crucifixion can be saved. There, in the space between heaven and earth, in the liminal space, Jesus became your Saviour, your *axis mundi.*

How does this relate to the trauma you have suffered? At the time when Christ suffered and died on the cross, He entered the liminal space and built a bridge between heaven and earth through His death and resurrection. He interceded on humanity's behalf and made kingdom integration possible. We are intended to live lives filled with righteousness, joy and peace. God wants his children who have suffered trauma to remember that the Holy Spirit can assist them towards self-integration, even after the fragmentation of trauma has caused them immense confusion and emotional chaos. Revisiting and accepting Christ's sacrifice on the cross for the trauma that you have experienced, will allow you to experience emotional safety and stability again. The Lord wants you to feel good about yourself, and the world you live in. He desires that you have a balanced life, with Him at the centre.

In today's art-making directive, you will create art and reflect on Christ as the centerpiece of your full salvation. In addition to that, you are invited to revisit Him as your *Axis Mundi,* amid your traumatic experience. Like the cross on the hill, you will place the crucified Christ's cross in the middle of the critical incident that has caused you to suffer so much emotional wounding.

Invitation to pray, breathe and contemplate

- Draw your attention to the earth underneath your feet. Feel what it feels like to be solidly anchored.
- Breathe slowly and pull any scattered senses together. Once you feel emotionally settled, anchor your thoughts on God.
- Shift your attention to the Person of Jesus Christ.
- Welcome Holy Spirit into this session with you.
- Meditate on how it feels to be anchored in the Lord. Remind yourself of his full humanity when He became your Saviour and Mediator. Jesus did not only care for your salvation, he desires for you to live a life filled with abundance, in the same way your soul prospers. He knows about the awful traumatic experience that has been haunting you. He is interceding on your behalf before the Father's throne.
- Contemplate his role as your heavenly mediator, interceding for you in the court of heaven.
- When you feel cemented and anchored, with your mind fixed on Christ, breathe slowly in and out and begin with the following reflective artmaking activity.

Artmaking directive

While keeping your breathing slow and regulated,

- Bring to attention the view of what you think it would have looked and felt like when Jesus was on the cross. Was it cold? Was it dark? Was it silent?
- With your non-dominant hand, draw the image of the cross in your journal or the canvas.
- Now, with your breath still controlled, shift your attention to the traumatic incident that you have experienced. What image comes to mind when you think about it? What do you see? Who is with you? Where were you? How old were you? What clothes did you wear? What does it feel like?
- On another page or canvas, and with your dominant hand, draw your dominant hand. Draw an image of the pain incident that has been hurting you for so long. Notice what you feel and think while you are working on the art. Look at it.
- You know have two images: One art image is about Jesus's cross. The other is an image representative of the pain story in your life.
- Slowly and deliberately place the image of pain behind the image of Jesus' cross. Make sure that the cross completely covers the trauma.
- Draw your attention to the sensations in your body when these two images collide.
- Imprint the picture of Jesus's cross overshadowing the trauma image as the central focus of your awareness.
- Close your eyes and sit with that image for a while. While doing that, place one hand on your heart and the other on the place where you might feel some sensation in your body.
- Breathe slowly and thank Jesus who was able to separate you from that trauma.
- Sit with this awareness until you feel a shift in your body. Once you feel stable and emotionally able, you can open your eyes.

DR ANNA DOS SANTOS

Observation

It is a profound experience when you become aware that Jesus Christ, who is the same, yesterday, today and forever, can be brought into your trauma in such a real way, particularly when the two images are brought together to become one. Stay with this creative process until you are convinced that your mind has carved this image into your memory for good. When you are done, you can pack your art material away.

Reflection time

Permit yourself to look without judgement, at the image you have created. Look with intent, as if you are seeing it for the first time. Observe your emotions, the sensations in your body, and your thoughts while doing that.

Ask yourself

What do I see? What thoughts come to mind when you look at your image?

- Which emotions come to mind when you look at the image of the cross that invaded the trauma? What colour did you use for the cross? Which colours surrounded the cross?
- Try to remember how your body felt when you created this image. Are there any new sensations in your body that you become aware of now that you are looking at it again?
- Are there any colour, shapes, or patterns that stand out from the trauma feelings and image you have created? What are they and what do you think about them?
- Do some aspects of the art image cause you to linger? What are they and what else comes to mind when you look at it?
- Now that you revisit the combined art piece, is there something you want to change? If necessary, adjust it and then look at the art image again. How do you feel now that you have altered it?
- If you could give a name or title to the image, what would it be? Write the title onto the artwork.

Journaling

Write down any thoughts and feelings, awareness or questions that might come to mind when you contemplate moving and positioning the critical incident that happened behind Jesus's cross.

- What do you feel when you think about now that Christ is in this image? Do any other thoughts or questions come to mind? It is ok to question God, He is not afraid of your inquiries. Write them down. Father God is delighted when we are curious about Him and his plans for us.

Neuroscience Fact

When a person revisits a memory about an incident that happened in the past and something gets altered in the image of the memory, something happens. Once an image in the brain has been modified through additional information or imagery, the memory about that image gets upgraded. It can never be the same. The image of Jesus's cross, placed in that memory of your pain and suffering has changed the original memory. The altered image is now engraved in your memory bank. You are no longer alone in that situation. Jesus, on the cross, or resurrected is with you, also in that memory. He has shared your pain, and you can surrender it to Him. By engaging with the artmaking reflection this way, you have given Jesus the permission to not only be a witness of the unrighteousness that has been done to you, but you also allowed him to carry it on your behalf. Sit with the thought and reflect on that for a while.

- Permitting for self-compassion and kindness in the days after you have done this art reflection is important. Remember, re-entering and revisiting a scene of pain and trauma is not easy. You used a lot of emotional energy and courage to do so. Allow yourself some time for physical and emotional relaxation after this intense session.

- Close the session with an intimate prayer. Speak to your Heavenly Father who loves you. Share with Him how you feel about Jesus whose cross now overshadows your trauma. Ask Holy Spirit to minister to your soul for the night and the days to come. End this session with thanksgiving and praise for our Creator God who loved you so much that He gave us His Son. His stripes and suffering paid the prize for your trauma to be healed. Following is a poem that I wrote about Jesus in this liminal space.

The Liminal Space

Life is old there, older than the trees.
The liminal space in the in-between, flanked by what was and is next.
We live there all the time—that middle ground between two grounds.
The transitional space. The void where I must let go, yet I remain.
The threshold where I want to change but still keep on the same
I long for a sacred space where everything transforms so I can move on.
Life is old there.

Jesus in the Liminal Space
Life is precious there, older than the trees.
On the cross in the liminal space, flanked by what was and what is to come.
Christ died there, once and for all—in the middle between heaven and hell.
The void has been closed in the transitional space.......
I can let go.
The threshold where I change without having to change anything myself.
That sacred space where everything transforms, and He remains.
Life is new here.

Anna Dos Santos

GENESIS, DAY THREE

Fruit According to Its Kind

Then God said, "Let the waters under the heavens be gathered together into one place, and let the dry land appear and it was so. And God called the dry land Earth, and the gathering together of the waters He called Seas. And God saw that it was good. Then God said, "Let the earth bring forth grass, the herb that yields seed, and the fruit tree that yields fruit according to its kind, whose seed is in itself, on the earth,". And it was so. And the earth brought forth grass, the herb that yields seed according to its kind, and the tree that yields fruit, whose seed is in itself according to its kind. And God saw hat it was good. So the evening and the morning were the third day
(Genesis 1: 9 – 13).

Meditate

During the previous interventions you have learned how to ground yourself and reflect on God's character. You also brought one critical incident that caused you great harm to the forefront. You then allowed that space to be invaded by Christ's presence and the image of him crucified. You will do well to hold onto those grounding images and reflections for the rest of your life. It is an excellent way to align yourself around the foundational truth of who God is, and what He has done for you. This helps to provide emotional stability when you feel insecure or anxious. Being anchored in God's character is foundational for emotional stability when you desire to reaffirm your identity and destiny.

God continued His magnificent creative work on Day 3. He provided the earth with seeds, plants and trees, and then commanded them to reproduce and multiply, each after their own kind. As God's creature whom He placed on this earth, you also have the potential to increase in all the domains where you exist and function. But people who suffer from the after-effects of trauma find being productive difficult. This is because the chaos of emotional wounding results in them no longer remembering their worth, what they like or who to trust. Yes, trauma has caused them to lose sight of their ability to produce, enjoy life and multiply the fruit of their labours.

Our garden in South Africa was filled with different fruits. In the summer we enjoyed the luxury of avocados, peaches, lemons, apricots, papayas and grapes. To produce good fruits, trees must be cared for and managed well. Not only do they need good soil and water, but they also must be pruned wisely to produce the best fruit possible. Good tending implies that trees must be inspected and assessed to determine what needs to be done for the orchard to produce lavishly in the next season. This resonates when we think about self-care. Without proper self-management and applicable self-nurturing, people can't prosper or grow in their mental or emotional health. Your life has multiple layers and life domains. How you engage with and function in those domains is paramount if you want to repair trauma chaos and damage. For the next reflection, you will revisit the different life domains where you function to self-assess how trauma has impacted you and then proceed to plan for proper self-care, emotional growth, and self-integration.

Reflection intention

This art directive will help you assess most of the domains of existence you inhabit and function in. Below is a summary of these domains and you are invited to prayerfully explore how you think you manifest and show up in each domain. The goal of the intervention is to learn more about yourself and your engagement in the world and to determine how trauma has stolen your joy to engage in each life domain.

Grounding meditation

- Breathe slowly in and out. Pull your five senses together. Listen to the sounds around you. Is there silence or do you hear something? What is it?
- Feel the ground under your feet and the soft air on your cheeks.
- What do you smell?
- What taste is in your mouth?
- Visualize your breath flowing through your entire body. Centre your thoughts on God your Creator who has breathed His breath into your nostrils, the same way He did with Adam and Eve in the Garden of Eden.
- Anchored on the thought of the Creator whose Spirit provided you life, shift your attention to the person of Jesus Christ, also described in the Book of Revelation as the *Tree of Life*. Imagine the Tree of Life, life-giving and magnificent in the middle of the Garden of Eden. Meditate on this beautiful image for as long as you need to. Now, I want to draw your attention to Holy Spirit, who can bubble up inside of you like a well of living water. Imagine yourself as a tree that grows in this lovely garden close to the Tree of Life. Through grace, you are alive and welcomed into this garden again. You too can draw water from the well and be sustained... Once you can own, and feel part of this scene, you are ready to engage with the following reflective artmaking activity.

Artmaking Directive

- With your non-dominant hand, draw an image of the Tree of Life.
- When you are done with the tree, you will continue with artmaking to create a garden for that tree to grow in. Because this is your garden that you will work on, you can use your dominant hand to create the garden. Before you commence to populate the garden, you need to familiarize yourself with the

different trees and plants that will grow in the garden. Below is an introduction to each of your life domains, that you will represent as a tree or a plant.

The diagram introduces the different life domains where we function as humans. Please review it and imagine each domain is a different tree for your garden. Create an image of each tree. Remember to indicate whether your tree produce fruit or flowers.

Your Multi-level Life Domains

- While keeping your breathing slow and regulated, please review and explore each life-domain.
- Imagine these domains as individual trees that are to grow alongside the Tree of Life in your garden.
- Think how each tree or plant would look like, if it is planted in the garden. Draw a different tree for each domain and place it in the garden. The domains you will revisit are:
- **The Divine domain**: This is your relationship and connection with God. This includes how you worship. Worship is an active physical manifestation where we acknowledge God, who dwells in the invisible world we can't see, but also indwells.
- **Your Psyche (Soul)**: Your emotional and mental domain: What is the health status and connection between what you feel, think and do? Do your emotions and thoughts resonate with each other? Can you feel, acknowledge and manage your feelings?
- **Intimacy and belonging**: How connected and seen do you feel as it relates to your significant other?
- **Relationship with self/others**: How connected and healthy are your relationships with others in your family, with friends, colleagues, in society and community (This includes your church community)?
- **Physical Health**: How healthy are you? What does your sleep hygiene look like? Do you exercise enough? How much water do you drink daily?
- **Connection with nature and your environment**: How often do you spend time in nature? Do you care about the environment? Is your living space organized and clean?
- **Career/Employment**: How much do you care for and enjoy your work?
- **Finances**: Do you manage your finances well? This does not mean that you have to be rich to have a good tree, no, it means that you know how to budget and that you can stay within your budget.
- **The Future**: Do you have hope for the future? Do you have a dream? Do you know what you want to do to live that dream?
- Spend as much time as needed to create a tree for each domain.

Contemplation Reflection

By placing each tree alongside the Tree of Life in your imaginary garden, you are now ready to engage with the art. Pause, take a deep and slow breath.

- Permit yourself to look without judgement at the garden.
- Observe your emotions and the physical awareness of your body while doing that.
- Note your thoughts about this imaginary garden and the domains of your life.
- Contemplate the many domains and how you connect and function in them.
- Because each is represented as a tree or a plant, you can now assess the status and health of every domain.
- How big is each tree in comparison with the Tree of Life?
- How close are these trees to one another?
- Which tree is the smallest? Why do you think it is so small?
- Which tree do you like the most?
- Which tree are you not satisfied with? Why?
- Begin with your journaling reflection when you are done. Write down any thoughts and feelings, awareness or questions that might come to the fore as they relate to the individual domains of your life.

Ask yourself the following questions

- What does your garden look like? Do you like it, or are there some domains /trees in the garden that cause you some concern?
- Which trees or domains leave you with a feeling of contentment?
- Is your garden safe and protected from the storms? Does it have enough water?
- Is it a healthy and growing garden?
- Is there any tree in the garden that needs more attention and loving-kindness? Which tree/domain is it? Remember to identify and name the domain without judgement, guilt, or criticism.

- Which life domains present as mature? Do your trees produce any fruit or flowers?
- Are you satisfied with the status of each tree?
- If you want to change some trees, you are welcome to do so.
- Once the garden has been fully visited, I invite you to add an image of the Tree of Life to your garden. You can draw and place it wherever you think it should be.
- Welcome the Tree of Life into your garden.

Disclaimer

A word of caution, do not judge the garden or the gardener too harshly. This garden and all its domains have experienced a recent storm. Also, all gardens need ongoing attention, pruning and maintenance. Because plants are different, we must remember that some plants are more sensitive to weather and wind than others. Each tree is unique and has different needs and requirements to flourish. Some plants require more attention than others. There are also different seasons. Trees and plants experience and react seasonally.

Prayer

Thank you, Heavenly Father for the richness and versatility of my life. That I am functioning in so many domains. Grateful, I bring my entire life and all its domains and surrender it to you, Jesus. Thank you for sending Holy Spirit to guide me daily. Holy Spirit, your guidance gives me comfort. Your wisdom will help and direct me in all my life's domains and dimensions. Thank you for showing me which of these domains needs attention. Please help me to become mindful and deliberate and tend to each facet of my life in a way that draws from the Tree of Life. In surrender, I bring my life domains to you Lord. This way, I will mature and grow, producing fruit in your kingdom. I offer this song from King David as a sacrifice of praise to you:

We shall be satisfied with the goodness of Your house, of Your holy temple.

By awesome deeds in righteousness You will answer us, O God of our salvation, You who are the confidence of all the ends of the earth, and of the far-off seas; who established the mountains by His strength, being clothed with power;

You who still the noise of the seas, The noise of their waves, and the tumult of the peoples.

They also who dwell in the farthest parts are afraid of Your signs; You make the outgoings of the morning and evening rejoice.

You visit the earth and water it, You greatly enrich it; The river of God is full of water; You provide their grain, for so You have prepared it.

You water its ridges abundantly, You settle its furrows; You make it soft with showers, You bless its growth.

You crown the year with Your goodness, and Your paths drip with abundance.

They drop on the pastures of the wilderness, and the little hills rejoice on every side.

The pastures are clothed with flocks; The valleys also are covered with grain; They shout for joy, they also sing. Amen (Psalm 65:4-13).

GENESIS - DAY FOUR

Signs and Seasons for Enlightenment

Then God said, "Let there be lights in the firmament of the heavens to divide the day from the night; and let them be for signs and seasons, and for days and years, and let them be lights in the firmament of the heavens to give light on the earth"; and it was so. Then God made two great lights the greater light to rule the day and the lesser light to rule the night. He made the stars also. God set them in the firmament of the heavens to give light on the earth, and to rule over the day and over the night, and to divide the light from the darkness. And God saw that it was good. So the evening and the morning were the fourth day

(Genesis 1:14-19)

Meditation

During your art reflection about Day Three, you had the opportunity to name and engage with the different domains where you function. Exploring Day Four of the Creation story, we see that God, by creating the sun, moon and stars to support the earth and its inhabitants, imbedded continuity, and chronological seasonality into the fabric of humanity's existence. By experiencing predictability, balance, clarity, equilibrium, and spatiality during our life cycles, God teaches us that we live within seasons, structures, systems, and cycles. This provides us with a sense of belonging. He also desires that we learn to discern between periods of joy and suffering and embrace each of these seasons as important and part of a life that can be lived well.

The sun and the moon made these seasons possible. The sun provides the Earth with life-giving heat and energy and holds our entire solar system together. Due to its 23.45 degrees off-kilter tilted axis, the

Earth remains directed towards the sun. The moon is also important. It provides us with gravity. Without gravity, the Earth's tilt would not be stable, and when we rotated around the sun, the Earth would quiver continuously! Like the earth which cannot exist without the sun, we need God. He is our constant sustainer and protector throughout our entire life story. This provides us with a sense of belonging. He also desires that we learn to discern between periods of joy and suffering and embrace each of these seasons as important and part of a life that can be lived well. That is why we need the moon also, as its gravity provides us with each season and protects us from the sun's direct heat.

Trauma shakes the predictability of our lives and can affect a person's entire personhood and how they interact with life. When a person experiences a traumatic event, not only do their memories get distorted, but they are also totally disoriented! Think about it this way, when a colourful string of beads is suddenly cut, beads will fall and scatter everywhere. Collecting all the beads takes time and patience. Trying to string them in the same original pattern is almost impossible! The same goes for our memories after trauma. They get fragmented. But there is even more damage. Trauma causes people to experience deep shame, and it makes it difficult for people to engage in intimate relationships with others. Van Der Kolk says, "Deep down many traumatized people are even more haunted by the shame they feel about what they did or did not do under the circumstances. They despised themselves for how terrified, dependent, excited, or enraged they felt."[240]

To integrate and move towards a new normal, traumatized people need a restoration that includes order and stability, assisting the neurons to fire together, and form new thought patterns. Over time people own these new patterns which are included in such a way that they become newly established habits. This provides predictability. Predictability assists people in rebuilding an identity around what they know about themselves. New memories can be created, with a sense of self-worth around the patterns and habits they now inhabit.

Visiting Day Four of the Creation story, we celebrate the importance of seasonality. In the first verse of Ecclesiastes chapter 3, we read, "To

---

[240] Van Der Kolk, *The Body Keeps Score: Brain, Mind, and Body in the Healing of Trauma.* (Penguin Books, 2015).196.

everything, there is a season, A time for every purpose under heaven. Moving forward with the next art directive, you will revisit the different seasons of your life, and how they played out over time. Gaining insight into the bigger picture of your life will help you acquire a different perspective and appreciation of who you are and everything you have experienced and encountered over your lifespan.

Prayer

Thank you Lord that,

"To everything there is a season, A time for every purpose under heaven: A time to be born, And a time to die; A time to plant, And a time to pluck what is planted; A time to kill, And a time to heal; A time to break down, And a time to build up; A time to weep, And a time to laugh; A time to mourn, And a time to dance. A time to cast away stones, And a time to gather stones; A time to embrace, And a time to refrain from embracing; A time to gain, And a time to lose; A time to keep, And a time to throw away; A time to tear, And a time to sew; A time to keep silence, And a time to speak; A time to love, And a time to hate; A time of war, And a time of peace. What profit has the worker from that in which he labours? I have seen the God-given task with which the sons of men are to be occupied. He has made everything beautiful in its time. Also, He has put eternity in their hearts, except that no one can find out the work God does from beginning to end."

Ecclesiastes 3:1-11.

'God of all seasons who rules over the seasons of my life, also over periods of darkness and pain, I turn my mind and gaze to you. Thank you for the time to pause and be still in your presence. I rejoice because I belong in your kingdom. I choose to bring all my life seasons in remembrance before you. Please help me to reflect with wisdom and discernment about the seasons of my life. I allow my soul to sink into your protection and abiding love. Guide me when I create art and reflect on the times and seasons of suffering. Holy Spirit whisper to my soul what you want me to know and understand about these times. Please help me to accept what you want me to understand. As I proceed with this art-making reflection, I open my ears to hear what you want me to hear, see what you want me to see, and feel what you want me to feel. I surrender my heart to yield to your will. Amen.'

Art Directive

- With this activity, you are invited to draw to explore and contemplate the different seasons in your life.
- Start by dividing the canvas, or an empty page into four sections. The sections can be placed in a circle or a square on the page or canvas. Identify each section as a season, namely Spring, Summer, Autumn and Winter. Decide what colour fits each season.
- Now, starting at the top or bottom of another empty page in your journal, draw a straight line across the entire page. This line will symbolize your lifeline.
- Beginning at your conception or your birth, jot any noteworthy experience down. While contemplating the different important experiences over your life span, note their impact or the thoughts or feelings you have about these encounters. If it is a positive experience, designate the colour that befits the emotional encounter you had during the experience. If it was a painful experience, allocate a colour that reminds you of winter or the negative feelings you experienced at the time.
- To describe the feelings or thoughts you experienced, write one or two words about them. Noteworthy, these experiences must cover both good and painful memories or encounters you have experienced. Take your time to complete this activity.
- Once the lifeline is done, turn your attention to your canvas or your art journal. This time you will need a big surface to work on. A big poster-size paper will work well.

- The goal for this part of the reflection is to allocate a place for each life experience you have experienced. You will do it in such a way that it fits into the specific season where it should be. If drawing images of each experience will take too much time, you can create a collage. Page through a few magazines and find pictures representing the experiences you have externalized at the beginning of this intervention. Glue each photo of the life encounter or experience onto the allocated season where it fits. Another way is by using different colours on different textures of paper, writing keywords down, and then adding it to the season where it fits. Complete the artwork and set the image apart to reflect on the seasons of your life.

Contemplation Reflection

- Notice that each season had unique challenges and life lessons you could learn from. God allowed the seasons of waiting, growing, multiplication, and pain. Each had a different purpose. Can you identify some of those purposes? If so, write them down.
- What colour did you allocate to each season? Why?
- Invite the art image of the cross, from the art you have created for Day 2's reflection, to be placed in the season of suffering.
- Reflect on what it means to no longer be alone, but to have Christ crucified with you in those dark moments of the winter season.
- Which season are you experiencing now?
- Which season occupied the most space on the canvas?
- Which season got the most attention?
- Which season do you think needed more loving-kindness?
- Finally, review your art and write a reflection about your life seasons. Do not be surprised when these thoughts come out in rhythmic patterns. If so, dedicate this poem as a prayer to the Lord.

Closing

In the wake of emotional trauma, something happens in the brain when externalized life encounters are identified and re-created as images which are categorized as seasons. When this happens, fragmented and disorganized thought patterns are addressed and re-organized. Thinking about life encounters in the context of spring, summer, autumn and winter provides a bigger context and purpose to the different experiences over your lifetime. Inviting Christ crucified into all the seasons in your life, helps to form a new cohesive story about your life. By externalizing and acknowledging that God is aware of, and could identify with your pain, a new story emerges. By doing this art reflection you will experience that trauma wounding is no longer scattered as hurtful fragments all over your brain. The season of emotional wounding was identified and localized. Once there is a boundary around the painful event, it becomes manageable, and life can return to a new rhythm with other seasons that you can participate in.

GENESIS - DAY FIVE

Sea Creatures and Every Winged Bird

Then God said, "Let the waters abound with an abundance of living creatures, and let birds fly above the earth across the face of the firmament of the heavens." So God created great sea creatures and every living thing that moves, with which the waters abounded, according to their kind, and every winged bird according to its kind. And God saw that it was good. And God blessed them, saying, "Be fruitful and multiply, and fill the waters in the seas and let birds multiply on the earth." So, the evening and the morning, were the fifth day.

(Genesis 1:20-23)

One of the first questions people ask me after they have encountered trauma, is, "Why did it happen to me? Why do I feel emotionally overwhelmed and anxious all the time?" This desperate question, coming from a believer is entirely reasonable, because it is certainly not God's will for them to suffer like this. He does not want his children to constantly experience anxiety, fear, anger or distrust of others. Nor does he want them to feel hopeless and without dreams for the future. We know that trauma affects people's body, soul and spirit, and can strike any time. So why does trauma happen? The answer is not singular or simple. Let us go to the Bible for answers. Throughout the biblical history of the Hebrew people, we read stories of how God intervened to address their trauma and anguish, which was often caused because of sin and disobedience to Him. Sometimes, it was because of sin, curses, his children's actions, or their inactions. So, believers can assume that trauma happens because of what we have done or refrained from doing, or else, what others have done to us. Trauma results when the consequences of these actions or inactions leave you in a state of fear, without any say or control to change the situation. Intergenerational trauma happens when the suffering of one generation is transferred to at least three or four generations to come. Some form of trauma that we often overlook, is when our spirit gets wounded. Day 5's reflection will include reflection on the wounded spirit's trauma. Our spirit, which comes from God, perceives intuitively. The human spirit is existential and connects us to the world around us.

Spirit-wounding often happens to unborn babies when the mother experiences severe trauma. Even though the frontal part of the brain has not fully developed yet, the baby's spirit is alive because it was activated at conception by God, who breathed His life into the baby. Because the baby's brain has not fully developed, the trauma happens without cognition of how it occurred, but the baby's spirit experienced the trauma. So, without the cognition to rationalize the trauma, the baby's spirit will respond accordingly and own the trauma's effect. Because the spirit exists in multiple dimensions, and as the brain continues to develop, the awareness about the trauma continues to prevail in the baby's subconscious as if it is continuously happening. That spirit wounding seems unending and later forms part of the person's selfhood. Let us see how this should be addressed.

On day five of the Creation story, God introduces us to two dimensions of existence, and he blessed both with life and multiplication. They are the sea and the heavens above. The earth's oceans cover two-thirds of its entire surface. The sea creatures playing in the deepest, darkest parts of the Earth, were to multiply and fill the oceans. Surrounding Earth is the heavens. The beautiful blue sky was to be filled with every winged bird, according to its kind. They were gorgeous and marvellous to behold. But what happens if the creatures that inhabit these two dimensions become dangerous? What if they begin to attack and destroy not only their habitat but also the earth in the middle?

For most of our existence, we simultaneously engage consciously and subconsciously with the world we live in. Your subconsciousness is the hidden part of your soul or psyche and contains the secrets of your heart. What you think, feel and dream, are birthed in your soul. Your psyche contains your subconsciousness which is like the ocean. It is filled with images, thoughts, feelings, memories and dreams. These thoughts, feelings and emotions can multiply, whether you want them to or not, it will happen. For example, if you hide a secret fear, it will remain in the dark, but it continues to grow and will eventually manifest. You will notice this in your heart. Job said, "For the thing I greatly feared has come upon me, and what I dreaded has happened to me." (Job 3:25) When fear grows, it takes over and eventually controls your entire life.

We can harbour many other secrets in the deep recesses of our hearts as well. For example, our hurt can breed unforgiveness or anger. Unforgiveness can become resentment. Resentment can turn into bitterness. Bitterness can grow to become hate. Anger can turn into wrath and revenge. Insecurity feeds off inferiority. The list goes on and on. Negative thoughts and feelings can multiply. Eventually, it will manifest in the body. These painful thoughts and feelings reveal themselves as brain patterns and could eventually erode every healthy endomorph in your brain. Later there is no serotonin or dopamine left to help you make choices or engage with life healthily. The opposite is also true, if you allow wholesome thoughts, filled with gratitude and joy, it can change your endorphins and you can begin to feel better, and think more positive thoughts.

There is another dimension where we also co-exist. That is the heavenly dimension. We can equate the heavens with the spiritual realm, where there is also activity. On Day 5 we see that the creatures of the heavens also multiply. According to Scripture, we know that there is always activity in the spiritual realm and not all this activity is necessarily good. Firstly, angels are operating in the heavenly sphere. We read, "He makes His angels spirits, and His ministers a flame of fire" (Hebrews 1:7). The Lord has commanded these angels or messengers to assist his children. See, "Are not the angels ministering servants designated to help us when we need assistance" (Hebrews 1:14). Apart from angels there are also evil spirits at work in the unseen heavenly realm. Satan has charge over them and they are sent to harass us. Believers are taught that our fight here on earth is not against people, but against evil in the atmosphere. We read, "For our struggle is not against flesh and blood, but against the rulers, authorities, powers of this world's darkness, and spiritual forces of evil in the heavenly realms" Ephesians 6:12. How does this relate to trauma?

When we reflect on Job's story of trauma, we see that Satan attempted to hurt Job so deeply that he would turn his back on God.

Sometimes trauma happens to us, not by our own doing, but because of evil intent. When that happens, we can either decide to turn our back on God, or we can determine to run to God. The choice is entirely ours. Job experienced trauma in all the dimensions and domains of his life. Yes, his body, soul and spirit were under attack. But like Job you are reminded that "The Name of the Lord is a strong tower; the righteous run into it, and are safe" (Proverbs 18:10).

What is the source of the trauma that you have suffered? How are you responding to it? Do you think trauma has caused you to harbour thoughts that do not benefit you? Have these negative thoughts succeeded in taking over your thought life and do you feel controlled by them? Do you discern that you are in a battle that is going on in the heavenly sphere? It is time to acknowledge these two dimensions, name what is happening, and address the issues that have multiplied in your life. The good news is that you do not have to fear, for the Lord has redeemed you, He has summoned you by your name, and you are His (Isaiah 43:1). Yes, you have not received a spirit that makes you a fearful slave. Instead, you have received God's Spirit when he adopted you as his own child. Now you can call him "Abba Father" (Romans 8:15).

Invitation

In today's reflection, you are invited to discern what is taking place in the deep recesses of your heart that has been multiplying. If there is a hidden sin in your heart, you can admit and turn away from it. Remember, the Lord is faithful to forgive. "If we confess our sins, He is faithful and just to forgive us our sins and to cleanse us from all unrighteousness" (1 John 1:9). We have this assurance that, "Everyone who calls on the name of the Lord will be saved" (Romans 10:13-17). On the other hand, if there is an unrevealed or unchallenged curse over your life, whether it is personal, intergenerational or because of a stronghold from Satan, which has not been dealt with, the forces of darkness will continue to harass you. This must be dealt with. If not, trauma will continue to control your life story. In today's activity, you will make art to explore and reflect on these two dimensions. Once that is done, you can bring them in alignment with God's will for you for you to, "prosper as your soul prospers" (3 John 1:2).

Prayer

Let us pray with Hildegard von Bingen, "Holy Spirit, giving life to all life, moving all creatures, root of all things, washing them clean, wiping out their mistakes, healing their wounds, you are our true life. Luminous and wonderful, awakening the heart from its ancient sleep. Please shine your light on me. Reveal the deep secrets of my heart. Beam down with your holiness, your bright clarity, and reveal to me the motives of my heart, the fears embedded in my soul, (the wounds inflicted on my spirit). Instruct me, direct me, guide me to the light. "[241] Reflecting on the two dimensions where my subconscious and consciousness operate, Lord please show me where you work in my life. Father God, would you remind me of the ways in which I have sinned through negligence, weakness, or my deliberate fault. …I repent of these and turn away from them to be led by Holy Spirit, who I trust to teach me how to live according to the principles of your Word. Amen.

Art-making Directive

Prayerfully create art while meditating about the two dimensions of Day 5 as it is manifested in your life.

- *The sea*: Begin with the dimension of the ocean as a metaphor for your soul. What topic influences your thoughts most of the day? Does this topic control your thoughts and internal dialogue? Identify the main idea or thought that comes to mind and, with your dominant hand, create an image about the topic.
- While busy with artmaking about the main theme of your daily thoughts, notice and observe the feelings that come to the

---

[241] Hildegard von Bingen. A 12th-century German writer and Benedictine abbess (1098 – 1179) in Star, M. Ed. *Devotions, Prayers and Living Wisdom*. Boulder: Sounds True, 2012.

surface as they are linked to the main thought, belief or idea you have identified to control your internal dialogue.

- Identify and name the feeling. Please remember that a feeling is not right or wrong. It just is. It is always important to notice which emotions manifest, but I suggest you don't allow these feelings to control you because they are fleeting and can change as your mood or thoughts change.
- Choose one colour for each feeling and create a pattern or image for each feeling in the art you are making about the image around the theme of your thoughts.
- How do these thoughts and feelings manifest? Do you have a specific behaviour as a result of the controlling thoughts and feelings? Draw an image of that. Set the image aside and move to the second dimension.
- *The heavens above*: If you have observed trends and patterns of trauma happening in your life or the life of your family, do some research and seek evidence of the possibility of iniquity or a family curse.[242] If so, create art about that. Use your non-dominant hand for this art-making. Once done with this art activity, book an appointment with your accountability partner to pray over and renounce the curse. A curse mostly comes because of sin against another, innocent blood that was spilled, or rebellion which is like witchcraft.[243]

Reflection

Put your art utensils aside when you are done with the art-making activity. Place the image a distance away and have a good look at it. If the image reveals some hidden sin or secret you feel ashamed of, get rid of the shame and guilt through the following prayer: "Father God, I take these moments to confess my sins before you now..."

---

[242] Robert Henderson. *Operating in the Courts of Heaven. Granting God the Legal Rights to Fulfill His Passion and Answer Our Prayers.* (Shippensburg, PA: Destiny Image Publishers, 2021)165 -183.

[243] 1 Samuel 15:23; 2 Chronicles 33:6; 2Kings 9:22; Micah 5:12,13; Nahum 3:4; Galatians 5:20-26.

- Take some time to name the sin, hiding in the darkness of your soul, to the Lord. "God of grace and mercy, thank you that when I confess my sin, You are faithful and just, forgiving and purifying me from all unrighteousness. (1 John 1:9). I receive your forgiveness now. Thank you that your light shines in the darkness, and the darkness can never extinguish it" (John 1:5).
- If you sense that the trauma is an attack from Satan, you need to re-armour yourself with the full armour of God so that you may be able to stand against the wiles of the devil. This is a process and requires serious time to reflect upon. While reflecting, you are invited to create art about each part of the armour that the Lord wants you to wear, and what it implies for your life during this season when Satan is attacking you or your loved ones. Here is the armour:

> *Put on the whole armour of God, that ye may be able to stand against the wiles of the devil. For we wrestle not against flesh and blood, but against principalities, against powers, against the rulers of the darkness of this world, against spiritual wickedness in high places. Therefore take unto you the whole armour of God, that ye may be able to withstand in the evil day, and having done all, to stand. Stand therefore, having your loins girt about with truth, and having on the breastplate of righteousness; And your feet shod with the preparation of the gospel of peace; Above all, taking the shield of faith, wherewith ye shall be able to quench all the fiery darts of the wicked. And take the helmet of salvation, and the sword of the Spirit, which is the word of God: Praying always with all prayer and supplication in the Spirit, and watching thereunto with all perseverance and supplication for all saints;*
>
> Ephesians 6:11-18.

Self-reflection

Write your reflections, and what you have discovered about these two dimensions in your journal. Spend enough time with this reflection. This is a very sacred and personal process. Once done, it is important that you discuss Day 5's experience and encounter with your accountability partner and have them pray with you about it. We need a witness to journey with us when we address these deep dimensions of our soul. Finally, I invite you to pray with the writer of Jude: "Now unto Him who is able to keep you from stumbling, and to present you faultless before the presence of His glory with exceeding joy, to our God and Saviour who alone is wise, be glory and majesty, dominion and power, both now and forever. Amen." (Jude 16, NKJ)

Closing

Declare Psalm 46: 2 over your life: 'So we will not be afraid, even if the earth is shaken and mountains fall into the ocean depths.' Amen.

DAY 6

Let Us Make Man in Our Image:
Saying Hello Again

Then God said, "Let the earth bring forth the living creature according to its kind: cattle and creeping thing and beast of the earth, each according to its kind," and it was so. And God made the beasts of the earth according to its kind, cattle according to its kind, and everything that creeps on the earth according to its kind. And God saw that it was good. Then God said, "Let Us make man in our image, according to our likeness; let them have dominion over the fish of the sea, over the birds of the air, and over the cattle, over all the earth and over every creeping thing that creeps on the earth." So God created man in His own image, in the image of God He created him; male and female He created them. Then God blessed them, and God said to them, "Be fruitful and multiply; fill the earth and subdue it; have dominion over the fish of the sea, over the birds of the air, and over every living thing that moves on the earth. "And God said, "See, I have given you every herb that yields seed which is on the face of all the earth, and every tree whose fruit yields seed; to you, it shall be for food. Also, to every beast of the earth, to every bird of the air, and to everything that creeps on the earth, in which there is life, I have given every green herb for food,"; and it was so. Then God saw everything that He had made, and indeed it was very good. So the evening and the morning were the sixth day.

(Genesis 1:24-31)

Meditation

God created humanity in His image, to fully engage with a life filled with purpose and divine destiny. We were made to reflect His glory, take care of, and have dominion over this beautiful earth that Creator God has created. Reflecting on this command and the blessing it entails for abundance rulership, surely must trigger a gratitude and worship response. Knowing and celebrating who you are and having an awareness of who God wanted you to be, is very important when trauma tries to derail your thoughts and emotions about your self-identity and self-worth. The purpose of the next reflection is to celebrate an act of reintegration of the fragmented self, which is intended to help with emotional balance and re-engagement with life. The purpose of Day 6's reflection is ultimately for you to say *Hello to yourself* again. Before you engage with the artmaking, please pray the next psalm with King David who reminded the Levite choir how precious they are in God's sight:

> *O Lord, You have searched me and known me.*
> *You know my sitting down and my rising up;*
> *You understand my thought afar off.*
> *You comprehend my path and my lying down,*
> *And are acquainted with all my ways.*
> *For there is not a word on my tongue,*
> *But behold, O Lord, You know it altogether.*
> *You have hedged me behind and before,*
> *And laid Your hand upon me.*
> *Such knowledge is too wonderful for me;*
> *It is high, I cannot attain it.*
> *Where can I go from Your Spirit?*
> *Or where can I flee from your presence?*
> *If I ascend into heaven, You are there;*
> *If I make my bed in hell, behold, You are there.*
> *If I take the wings of the morning,*
> *And dwell in the uttermost parts of the sea,*
> *Even there Your hand shall lead me,*

And Your right hand shall hold me.
If I say, "Surely the darkness shall fall on me,"
Even the night shall be light about me;
Indeed, the darkness shall not hide from You,
But the night shines as the day;
The darkness and the light are both alike to You.
For You formed my inward parts;
You covered me in my mother's womb.
I will praise You, for I am fearfully and wonderfully made;
Marvelous are Your works,
And that my soul knows very well.
My frame was not hidden from You,
When I was made in secret,
And skillfully wrought in the lowest parts of the earth.
Your eyes saw my substance, being yet unformed.
And in Your book they all were written,
The days fashioned for me,
When as yet there were none of them.
How precious also are Your thoughts to me, O God!
How great is the sum of them!
If I should count them, they would be more in number
than the sand;
When I awake, I am still with You.
Oh, that You would slay the wicked, O God!
Depart from me, therefore, you bloodthirsty men.
For they speak against You wickedly;
Your enemies take Your name in vain.
Do I not hate them, O Lord, who hate You?
And do I not loathe those who rise up against You?
I hate them with perfect hatred;
I count them my enemies.
Search me, O God, and know my heart;
Try me, and know my anxieties;
And see if there is any wicked way in me,
And lead me in the way everlasting.

Psalm 139.

Art Directive

You will create art about yourself. The easiest way is to make an image of your face. Once you have done that, you will sit with the image and reflect on the truth that God loves you exactly as you are. You are important to Him. He cares about you. Your name is engraved upon his heart.

- Take a comfortable position. Relax your entire body as much as possible. Sit still, close your eyes and breathe slowly and deeply. When you feel centred and grounded, you can continue with the artmaking.
- Use a hand mirror to look at your face. Look with intention. Explore your eyes, your nose, your mouth, and your face in its entirety. Feel with your fingers and hands what your face feels like.
- Look at each element of your face. Explore the five senses that it represents: Smell, taste, see, feel, hear.
- Once you have explored your face, create art about what you saw.
- You can try to draw your face exactly what it looks like in the mirror, or you can create an image of what you see when you look in the mirror. Create the image with loving-kindness, gentleness and joy. It can also be playful. No criticism about your appearance is allowed.

Reflection

- When the art is done, put your art materials and supplies aside. Place the image a distance away from you. Look at it.
- What do you see?
- Say hello to the image of you on the canvas. What does that feel like?
- What do you feel when you look at the image?
- What do you like when you look at each element of your face? For example, the eyes are the windows into your soul. What does it feel like to have a window into your own soul?

- What do you notice about yourself when you look at the image of your face?
- Is there something that you dislike about the art? If so, what is it and why?
- Is there something that you want to change about the art? If so, change it.
- How do you feel now that you have changed the image?
- Is there something that you want to say to the art? What is it?
- If the image could speak to you, what do you think, it would want to say to you?
- Write your name under the image.
- Welcome your image and thank God for bringing you to this world.

Blueprint Self-discovery (Not mandatory to do)

The purpose of the next activity is not directly related to trauma but could assist you in a rediscovery of who you are, what your life passion is, and what makes you authentically you. For this reflection, you must invest time and research your life history. The invitation is to draw a life map or -blueprint about yourself. The map will commence from the day, or even before, you were born, until you are about 19. (If you are younger than 19, work within the timeframe that you have.)

Some people will have much less than other people to reflect on. That is also good. Here are the directives.

- Open your journal on two clean pages. At the top of the first page, write: *My Life Blueprint.*
- Divide the two pages into two sections.
- On the left side, and in the first column, write about positive or enjoyable recollections you have about yourself throughout your lifespan. In the second column, write down why the memory is a good one, and why it was good. Continue reflecting on the positive memories until the age of 19. You can explore further if you want to do it. Here is an example of how to do the map:

My Life Blueprint

Name the delightful experience/Good Memory	Why was the experience good?
0 years: 4 years: 6 years: I got my first bicycle 7 years 8 years 9 years 10 years 11 years 12 years 13 years 14 years 15 years 16 years 17 years 18 years 19 years **Conclusion summary**	Dad taught me to ride. I love spending time with Dad I love adventure I am a person who loves adventure, and more than that, I absolutely love to share my life and the experiences that I have with the people that I love.

On the opposite page, create a record of your past from 0 to 19 years old. This time you are invited to reflect on the painful or negative experiences in your life history. Here is an example:

Negative Experience/ Painful Memory	Why was the experience painful and did you not like it?
0 years: 1 year: 2 years: 3 Years 4 years: Grandpa died 5 Years 7 years: Front teeth - 10 years: 11 years: 18 years: Motorbike accident - 19 years: ….. **Conclusion summary**: I suffered the loss of a secure attachment figure, and I learned to distrust people who rejected me because of my appearance. I suffered physical loss of mobility.	I mourned the loss of a person I deeply loved. I was bullied because of my appearance and was deeply hurt by the rejection I have experienced. I lost my mobility and the ability to explore new things, to feel speed…

You can write as much or as little as you want to about these events and experiences. When you are done with the mapping, you are invited to draw a map or a blueprint of your life experiences.

Reflection

Once you have completed both exercises, the invitation is to read through the entirety of both the positive encounters as well as the negative ones. From these experiences try to conclude who you are. Begin with the positive encounters. Try to determine and conclude who this person is who loved these different things in life. Write your findings as a summary down. Once you are done with this, move on to the other page. Do the same thing when you revisit the negative encounters. Why did you not like what has happened, and how did it impact you?

Reflect on both these columns and summarise them for yourself. By reading through it, determine how these events impacted your life, and who you became. Who do you think is the person that God had in mind when He allowed you to have fun and enjoy the gift of life? Include the things that caused you pain and ask yourself why these things hurt so deeply. Write a summary reflection about these thoughts as they relate to who you have become because of all your life experiences. When everything is said and done, the invitation is for you to reclaim the whole person back that God wanted you to be. Celebrate yourself. You have the divine right to reclaim your life back from pain and destruction. Satan might have tried to steal the truth from you, but the Truth will set you free. The Accuser will try to condemn and limit you. But, if you have repented from your sin, and have accepted Jesus as your Lord and Saviour, Satan has no legal right nor claim on your life. Jesus's broken body and blood have paid in full for your redemption. Every curse can be broken in Jesus' Name. Stand up and declare that into the atmosphere. God, is your Righteous Judge and He is presiding over the court of Heaven. Jesus Christ, sitting next to the Father, is your Mediator. The Saviour has given his life as a ransom for your restoration. You are an heir of the Father, and you can take your rightful place, and become who Father God intended you to be.

Pray

Heavenly Father, I want to praise and exalt your glorious Name, as your rulership is in heaven, let your kingdom and rulership come into my life here and now as well. You have always had a divine plan and a purpose for my life. I accept myself as a gift from you to this world. Thank you for creating me. I embrace myself as your gift and will value myself as you value me. I choose to love myself and I love you. In Jesus Name. Amen.

DAY 7: SHÂBBAT

Completion and Rest

Thus the heavens and the earth, and all the host of them, were finished. And on the seventh day, God ended His work which He had done and He rested on the seventh day from all His work which He had done. Then God blessed the seventh day and sanctified it, because in it He rested from all His work which God had created and made

(Genesis 2:1,2).

Contemplate

After processing your trauma through the stages and completing the art directives and reflections of the previous sessions, Day 7 is an invitation to rest. If you want to mirror entering the *Shâbbat* or rest of the Lord, as we read, He did in the Creation story, we see this rest as an invitation towards total surrender. Michael Fishbane describes *Shâbbat* as a sphere of inactivity. He says "One enters the sphere of inaction through divestment...Slowly, ... a sense of inaction takes over, and the day does not merely mark the stoppage of work or celebrate the completion of creation, but enforces the value that the earth is a gift of divine creativity, given to humankind in sacred trust...The Sabbath is thus a period of sacred stasis, a duration of sacred sanctity through the cultivation of inaction in body and spirit." [244] In the book of Hebrews, the writer talks about another rest. A rest away from striving to obtain salvation through works. He says, "There remains, a Sabbath-rest for the people of God; for anyone who enters God's rest also rests from their works, just as God did from his. Let us, therefore, make every effort to enter that rest, so that no one will perish by following their example

---

[244] Michael Fishbane, *Sacred Attunement: A Jewish Theology* (Chicago: Chicago Press, 2008), 125 -127.

of disobedience" (Hebrews 4:9,10). When I think about perfect rest, it implies total safety, which inevitably brings me to the well-known psalm of David as Eugene Peterson translated in The Message:

> God, my shepherd! I don't need a thing.
> You have bedded me down in lush meadows, you find me quiet pools to drink from.
> True to your word, you let me catch my breath and send me in the right direction.
> Even when the way goes through Death Valley,
> I'm not afraid when you walk at my side.
> Your trusty shepherd's crook makes me feel secure.
> You serve me a six-course dinner right in front of my enemies.
> You revive my drooping head; my cup brims with blessing.
> Your beauty and love chase after me every day of my life.
> I'm back home in the house of God for the rest of my life
> (Psalm 23).

Prayer

Lord, as you have rested, after you have created this world and all that is in it, I now want to declare that the work around the trauma I have experienced has been done. My day of rest has come. And so, in the quietness of this moment, I still my soul to spend this time with you.

"The day is yours, and yours also the night; you have prepared the light and the sun. You have set all the borders of the earth; you have made summer and winter" (Psalm 74:16,17). "I give thanks to You, O God, I give thanks! For your wondrous works declare that Your Name is near" (Psalm 75:1). Come Holy Spirit to my mind, I receive your rest in Christ. Come Holy Spirit to my heart, I receive your peace. Come Holy Spirit to my soul, I receive the Father's love for me. Amen.

Preparation for art-making

In preparation and in the stillness of the moment, close your eyes and focus on your breath.

- Try to relax and rest the muscles in your face, especially around your jaw and neckline. If it is comfortable, you can open your jaw slightly.
- Slowly inhale through your nose and exhale through your mouth. Listen to the regular sound of your breath.
- Relax all the muscles in your body. Start with your neck and shoulders. Now, relax the muscles in your arms, the palms of your hands and your fingers.
- Allow the breath to draw your attention to your back, over your chest, down to the centre of your body, your stomach, and all the way down to your spine and pelvis. Relax each part of your body as your breath moves over it.
- Let the feeling of relaxation and rest spread to your thighs, your knees and lower legs. Allow it to flow right down to your ankles and feet until it reaches the tips of your toes.
- Scan your entire body, starting at the top of your head down to your inner soles. Observe any part of your body that is still not relaxed.
- Identify and name the body part that does not feel relaxed. Take a deep breath and imagine the breath as warmth, light and kindness. Send this image to that part of your body that is still not at rest. When you exhale, imagine your breath carrying the tightness away to dissipate.
- Surrender yourself in this relaxed state to Holy Spirit.

Art-Directive

In reflection about what the rest of the Lord, away from trauma will look like for you, the invitation is to work within a circle or in three different circles. (A circle is often a sign of change or transformation). The art image you will create is intended to be a celebration. Before you start the artmaking, allow for a few minutes to meditate on how the Lord rested from his work. Think about what total rest will feel and look like for you.

- Draw one big circle or three circles of roughly the same size that touch each other.
- In the circle or circles, reflect and create an image of what total rest looks like if you experience it in your spirit, soul (or psyche) and your physical everyday life where you live, work, sleep and play.
- One circle can contain all these areas of rest, or the three circles can interconnect. It depends entirely on what you choose to do.
- Take as much time as you need to complete the art.
- Clean up and place your art so that you can have a good look at it.

Reflection

- What did you observe about yourself when you created art while meditating on entering God's rest?
- What items, surroundings or circumstances were important to make you feel rested, comfortable and nurtured?
- How did you decide what elements to include in your image?
- Why did you work within one circle or three separate circles?
- Now that you look at the image, is there anything that you think is missing?
- If so, what is it and why did you leave it out? If it is important, add it to the image.
- What colours did you use? Why? Which colours are missing?
- Does your image have a border? Why is it important or not important?
- Who would you love to share this image with?
- Choose a title for your image and write it down. Write any reflection or realization that came to mind about the art image.

In closing, well done. You were faithful to yourself and have responsibly worked through the chaos of emotional wounding and sorrow. You have completed a full circle.

Let us pray:

"As I enter prayer now, I pause to be still and reflect on the work that I have done over the past few weeks. I want to re-centre my attention upon your presence oh Lord. I choose to rejoice in Father God's creative love and abounding presence. Jesus, show me how to engage with the world from now on. I proclaim your beauty over my life, until every sorrowful story ends in joy. I join with the ancient praise of God's people: "May the nations praise you, O God. May all the nations praise you. Let the whole world sing for joy, because you govern nations with justice and guide the people of the whole world." (Psalm 67:3-4). Please light my soul on fire, keep me in a place of longing to stay in your eternal rest. Yes, I know that the emotional pain that I have suffered was real. But the blood of Jesus has given me a life beyond that pain. I am no longer defined by the trauma and defeat I have suffered. In following you Jesus, and by surrendering to your precious Holy Spirit I am learning to forget the things of the past and press on beyond to the empty cross towards you Jesus. What you have done for me is bigger than anything that has ever been done to me. Father, I receive the rest you have promised through Jesus's blood that was shed for me. I pray that I will know your rest and the freedom that will give me the authority to live a life filled with love, joy and peace. Holy Spirit show me how to carry Christ's love to the world. Help me to proclaim Christ in all I do and say. Amen."

SUMMARY AND CONCLUDING REFLECTIONS

Reading this book took you on a journey of discovery, creative artmaking and deep reflection about yourself and the emotional pain that you have encountered. It was not an easy choice and required much meandering and deep exploration. Doing that required courage and commitment. Not every person can do that. By working through each chapter of the book you have explored the impact of trauma and learned that its devastating effects are not only processed in your psyche and spirit but also stored in your body. Apart from the personal and relational damage, you learned that trauma also has an intergenerational effect that impacts societies generationally. By revisiting Job's story, in combination with knowledge gleaned from neuroscience about neuroplasticity, you discovered that effective trauma processing invariably enhances a person's life. Job was deeply traumatized when God invited him to the story of creation. But out of the whirlwind, God spoke to him, and Job rediscovered the Source of his existence, the reason why he does not have to fear. By revisiting the book of Genesis, you experienced how the story and process of how the world came into being, was used as a template to serve as the foundation for you to reclaim your life away from chaos back to wholeness. The rationale for using the Creation story for guidance to process trauma is such: If God was able to create such beauty and splendour in the physical world, his processes could certainly provide humanity with directives for restoration after trauma has fragmented their personhood and identity. That is why you were invited to engage with *Lectio Divina* reflections about the creation story, in combination with principles collected from phenomenological art therapy to implement your art-making reflections about the story of trauma in your life. Because you saturated your artmaking with prayer, Holy Spirit was able to guide and lead you on your reflections toward deep self-discovery and new insights that not only challenged but ultimately changed your thoughts and being.

Clinical studies have shown that trauma processing can be achieved through three definite phases. Firstly, a person must experience emotional acceptance, safety and grounding, before the second phase of thoughtful and thorough trauma processing and memory reconciliation can take place; The third phase of trauma work really begins when you engage with life again. So, after completing this book, you are encouraged to reconnect with others, particularly the community of believers in your city. Nothing can compare with the joy and blessing of worshiping the Lord in a community with other believers.

The directives and reflections about Scripture allowed for containment, emotional safety, and creative cognitive processing. Creating through tactile engagement, with visual imagery and externalized phenomena allowed you to experience somatic integration and an increasing self-awareness as it relates to your body's sensations. If a person is aware of what is going on in their body, what they feel and sense, it allows them more control over their body. This helps with tactile sense orientation, spatiality, and emotional engagement. You have also learned how to practice dual awareness. It means you know what it feels like to pendulate between emotional fragmentation and feeling emotionally stable. When the memories that originally caused great emotional turbulence, were processed, you aligned with the creative way how the story in Genesis played itself out procedurally. By processing these painful and fragmented memories at your own pace, your window of tolerance expanded, and your capacity to mentally shift states of awareness about the trauma toward memory reconciliation and integration grew. This will lead to an overall appreciation of well-being where you can celebrate life again. All the skills and information you have gleaned from working on your trauma story throughout the book, are not intended to be forgotten or stacked away somewhere in your memory bank. Please apply it to your life regularly.

Because there are not enough trauma-focused therapists in the world, many people do not have access to therapeutic services. On the other hand, some people do not have time, nor the means to travel far to work with an art therapist. The book emerged from a desire to assist some of these people of whom many are believers who suffer from the agony and pain of unprocessed trauma and who pray to the Lord for help. The creative format of the book, with its therapeutic artmaking directions, was designed with believers in mind who love to create art when they think and reflect on their lives.

Despite the possibility that the GENESIS approach could be controversial in the sense that it is a story taken from the Bible, I nevertheless have identified and provided reliable therapeutic interventions that can assist in effective trauma processing and memory reconciliation. In addition to its individual use, pastoral therapists facilitating trauma support groups will find that the latter part of the book can be used as a template for trauma processing. People contemplating the use of storytelling to assist in their art interventions and reflections will benefit from exploring the many other stories from the Bible when they need to find a way through a problem or an issue that causes them chaos or confusion.

To conclude, below is a summary of the Genesis model's approach to trauma processing. I hope that this framework will serve as a template to be utilized for the millions of believers who suffer from trauma symptoms. My heartfelt prayer is that you the reader, or any pastoral therapist who uses this book as a guide to facilitate workshops for trauma treatment, will experience the joy of witnessing how biblical principles applied, can redeem and restore people after trauma has stolen so much of their lives.

SUMMARY OF THE GENESIS APPROACH FOR TRAUMA TREATMENT

Phase One: Therapeutic Alliance, Safety, Assessment and Stabilization

Day One: The Principle of **Grounding** and Anchoring: *Safety and Stabilization.*

Day Two: The Principle of the believer's **Eternal Axis Mundi:** Our eternal existence in a relationship with God is because of Christ. The focus is on Liminality, Appropriation, Propitiation and Atonement.

Day Three: The Principle of **Nurturing and Responsible Self-care** in the different domains of our existence.

Phase Two: Trauma Processing and Trauma Memory Reconsolidation

Day Four: The Principle of **Endurance, Equipoise and Balance:** *Seasonality and Embodiment.*

Day Five: The Principle of **Spheres of existence:** *Multi-dimensional engagement with life, Allowing* for the *externalization of spirit, soul and body dimensions.*

Day Six: The Principle of **Identity Integration**: *Self re-integration, accepting responsibility.*

Phase Three: Integration and Post-Traumatic Growth

Day Seven: The Principle of **Shâbbat and Indwelling**: Entering God's rest. *Embracing and celebrating God's completed work of restoration.*

THE DEFINITION OF TERMS

This section defines important terms and concepts used throughout the book.

Diagnostic and Statistical Manual of Mental Disorders, **Fifth Edition, Text Revision (DSM-5-TR), 2022**, is the most comprehensive, current, and critical resource for clinical practice available to today's mental health clinicians and researchers and serves as the principal authority for psychiatric diagnoses in the United States and Canada. Treatment recommendations, as well as payment by health care providers, are often determined by DSM-5-TR classifications.

Heuristic Inquiry: This is "a type of phenomenological research that fully embraces, rather than brackets off, the personal insights of the researcher. The word "heuristic" comes from "eureka," meaning *"to discover"* or *"to find."* The defining characteristic of heuristic inquiry is the researcher's intentional use of self-awareness ... to discover new, in-depth meaning about an intensely experienced phenomenon."[245]

Phenomenological Art Therapy: Mala Betensky, who holds a phenomenological perspective of art therapy, underwrites an anthropo-philosophical view of humanity as "present-and future-oriented human beings-in-the-world" who are persons and not objects, "Each of them is a phenomenon with ... individually coloured innate qualities and propensities that make their relationships in their worlds highly

---

[245] Lynn Kapitan, *Introduction to Art Therapy Research*, 2nd ed. (New York & London: Routledge, Taylor, and Francis Group, 2018), 192.

individual."[246] Betensky states these phenomenological qualities are "intentionality, experiencing that involves all mental forces, consciousness, self-reflection, a need to create, and the striving for mental and spiritual growth throughout life."[247]

Poiesis: [ποίησις] is an ancient Greek word that means "the activity in which a person brings something into being that did not exist before." Hans Jauss explores the concept as aesthetic activity, with "the equating of producing with comprehending, which gives man access to truth through his poietic capacity." He further explains that *poiesis* "is the process in which aesthetic experience discovers the sphere of creative originality... *Poiesis* now means a process whereby the recipient becomes a participating creator of the work, [for example] [my poetry has the meaning one gives it]."[248] – Art therapy makes use of the principle of *poiesis*.

Tôhûw: is a Hebrew word used in Genesis one. The word originated "from an unused root that means "*to lie was*te; a desolation (of surface), i.e., desert; figuratively speaking: a worthless thing; when used as an adverb: in vain: confusion, empty place, without form, nothing, (think of) nought, vain, vanity, waste, wilderness."[249] In this book, the word alludes to a state of feeling and was mentioned in Chapter 5 in an individualized personal reflection.

Shâbath: is a Hebrew word used in Genesis 2:2. The prime root is "to *repose*, i.e., desist from exertion, used in causality, figurative speech of

---

[246] "Phenomena include visible, touchable, and audible things in the world around us, as well as thoughts and feelings, dreams, memories, fantasies, and all that stem from the human mind or spirit and belong in the realm of mental experiences. Employing the study of the consciousness, Husserl tried to reduce the perception of phenomena to their essence." Edmund Husserl, Ideas; 1913; 2nd ed. (N. J: Humanities Press,1976) in Mala G. Betensky, *What do you see? Phenomenology of Therapeutic Art Expression* (London: Jessica Kingsley Publishers, 1995), 3-4.

[247] Mala G. Betensky, *What do you see? Phenomenology of Therapeutic Art Expression* (London: Jessica Kingsley Publishers, 1995), xi.

[248] Hans Robert Jauss and Michael Shaw. "*Poiesis*" Critical Inquiry, Vol. 8, No. 3 (Spring, 1982), pp. 591-608. Published by: The University of Chicago Press. Accessed on May 31,2023. http://www.jstor.org/stable/1343267

[249] Strong, James, *Strong's Exhaustive Concordance* (Hendrickson Publishers, 2009),123.

specific. (cause to, let, make to) cease, celebrate, … suffer, to be lacking, leave, put away (down), (make) to rest, rid, still, take away."[250] The concept of *Shâbath* is used when it alludes to a state of being during a reflection after trauma processing has been completed. See Chapter 5.

Trauma: The concept of trauma is derived from the Greek word τραύμα which means wound, injury, or wounding and refers to a phenomenon that occurs after people have experienced emotional shock. The American Psychological Association defines trauma as "a deeply distressing or disturbing experience; or emotional shock following a stressful event or a physical injury, which may be associated with physical shock and sometimes leads to long-term neurosis."[251] Exposure to prolonged and untreated trauma can lead to different diagnoses as explained in the DSM-5-TR. Summarized, the symptom domains of Post Traumatic Stress Disorder are disturbances in self-organization as part of Complex PTSD; anxiety, depression, sleep problems, self-harm, dissociation, other physical, emotional, or social problems and substance abuse. The risk and protective factors assessed are stressful events, childhood trauma, history of mental illness, social support, and psychological resilience. [252]

---

[250] Ibid.,112.

[251] American Psychological Association "Trauma" Accessed on May 29, 2023. https://www.apa.org/topics/trauma

[252] American Psychiatric Association, *Diagnostic Statistical Manual of Mental Disorders Fifth Edition Text Revision,* DSM-5-TR. (Washington: American Psychiatric Association Publishing, Washington, DC. 2022.), 301- 312.

REFERENCES

Allen, Pat. B. *Art Is a Way of Knowing: A Guide to Self-Knowledge and Spiritual Fulfillment through Creativity.* Shambhala, 1995.

Ames, William. *The Marrow of Sacred Divinity, Drawne Out of the Holy Scriptures, and the Interpreters thereof, and brought into Method.* London: Edward Griffin for John à Rothwell at the Sun in Pauls-Church-yard. 1643.

American Psychiatric Association, *Diagnostic Statistical Manual of Mental Disorders Fifth Edition Text Revision,* DSM-5-TR. Washington: American Psychiatric Association Publishing, Washington, DC. 2022.

Amod, Z. Gericke, R and Bain, K. "Projective Assessment Using the Draw-A-Person Test and Kinetic Family Drawing in South Africa." In *Psychological Assessment in South Africa: Research and Applications*, edited by Sumaya Laher and Kate Cockcroft, 375–93. Wits University Press, 2013. https://doi.org/10.18772/22013015782.31.

Anderson, Ray. *On Being Human: Essays in Theological Anthropology.* Wipf & Stock Publishers, 2010.

Armstrong, Courtney. *Rethinking Trauma Treatment: Attachment, Memory Reconsolidation and Resilience.* New York. W.W. Norton & Company, 2019.

Badenoch, Bonnie. *The Heart of Trauma: Healing the Embodied Brain in the Context of Relationships.* W.W. Norton & Company, 2018.

Pope Benedict XVI in the post-synodal Apostolic Exhortation, *Verbum Domini* (nos. 86-87), accessed on February 2, 2023. https://www.vatican.va/content/benedict-xvi/en/apost_exhortations/documents/hf_ben-xvi_exh_20100930_verbum-domini.html

Brent Bezo & Stefania Maggi, 2015. "Living in "survival mode:" Intergenerational transmission of trauma from the Holodomor genocide of 1932–1933 in Ukraine. *Social Science & Medicine*, No.134, 87-94. 0277-9536. Accessed May 2023. https://doi.org/10.1016/j.socscimed.2015.04.009T.

Betensky, M.G. *What Do You See? Phenomenology of Therapeutic Art Expression*. Jessica Kingsley Publishers, 1995.

Bezo, Brent & Maggi, Stefania. "Living in "survival mode:" Intergenerational transmission of trauma from the Holodomor genocide of 1932–1933 in Ukraine. *Social Science & Medicine*, No.134, 2015.87-94. 0277-9536. Accessed May 2023. . https://doi.org/10.1016/j.socscimed.2015.04.009T

Bonhoeffer, D. *Creation and the Fall Temptation. Two Biblical Studies*. 2nd ed. Touchstone,1937.

Bowlby, J. (1982). Attachment and loss: Retrospect and prospect. *American Journal of Orthopsychiatry, 52*(4), 664–678. https://doi.org/10.1111/j.1939-0025.1982.tb01456.x

Bryan, Jocelyn. *Human Being: Insights from Psychology and the Christian Faith*. London: SCM Press, 2016.

Brewin, C.R., & Holmes, E.A. "Psychological theories of posttraumatic stress disorder." Clinical Psychology Review 23, no.3 (2003): 339–376, assessed Jan 12, 2023, https://doi.org/10.1016/S0272-7358(03)00033-3.

Briere, John N, and Catherine Scott. *Principles of Trauma Therapy: A Guide to Symptoms, Evaluation and Treatment*. 2nd ed. Los Angeles: Sage Publications, 2015.

Brockmeier, Jens. "From the End to the Beginning: Retrospective Teleology in Autobiography," In *Narrative and Identity: Studies in*

Autobiography, Self and Culture, ed. Jens Brockmeier and Donald Carbaugh. Amsterdam: Benjamins, 2001.

Bryan, Jocelyn. *Human Being: Insights from Psychology and the Christian Faith*. London: SCM Press, 2016.

Calhoun, L.G. & Tedeschi, R.G. *Facilitating Posttraumatic Growth: A Clinician's Guide*. New York: Taylor and Francis, 2008.

Calvin, J. (1536). *"Institutes of the Christian Religion,"* Book 2,1536. Assessed in November 2022, https://www.ccel.org/ccel/calvin/institutes.html

Canadian Art Therapy Association. https://www.canadianarttherapy.org/membership- levels/#registered.

Champagne FA. Early Adversity and Developmental Outcomes: Interaction Between Genetics, Epigenetics, and Social Experiences Across the Life Span. Perspect Psychol Sci. 2010. Sep;5(5):564-74. https://doi:10.1177/1745691610383494.PMID: 26162197.on humanity.

Congar, Yves. *The Spirit of God: Short Writings on the Holy Spirit.* (Washington, D.C.: Catholic University of America Press, 2018), 38. https://search-ebscohost- com.prov.idm.oclc.org/login.aspx?direct=true&db=nlebk&AN=1680073&site=ehost- live.

Cook, H. Christopher and Hamley, Isabelle. *The Bible and Mental Health: Towards a Biblical Theology of Mental Health* (London: SCM Press,2020), Dana, Deborah, A. *The Polyvagal Theory in Therapy: Engaging the Rhythm of Regulation*. W.W. Norton & Company, 2018.

Courtois, C. A. *Treatment of complex trauma: A sequenced, relationship-based approach* Guilford Press, 2015.

Currie, Mark. *About Time. Narrative, Fiction, and the Philosophy of Time*. Edinburgh: Edinburgh UP, 2007.

Davis, B.J. Ph.D. *Mindful Art Therapy: A Foundation for Practice*. Philadelphia, London: Jessica Kingsley, 2015.

Draaisma, Douwe. *Why Life Speeds Up as You Get Older: How Memory Shapes Our Past,* trans. Arnold Pomerans and Erica Pomerans. Cambridge: Cambridge University Press, 2004.

Dana, Deborah A. *The Polyvagal Theory in Therapy: Engaging the Rhythm of Regulation.* W.W. Norton & Company, 2018.

Entwistle, David N. *Integrative Approaches to Psychology and Christianity. An Introduction to Worldview Issues, Philosophical Foundations, and Modalities of Integration.* 3rd. Cascade Books. Eugene: Oregon, 2015.

Faith Alive Christian Resources, Christian Reformed Church. *Our Faith, Ecumenical Creeds, Reformed Confessions and Other Resources.* Grand Rapids: Michigan, 2013.

Farnsworth, K.E. "Conduct of Integration," *Journal of Psychology and Theology* no.10 (1982).

Fishbane, Michael. *Sacred Attunement: A Jewish Theology.* Chicago: Chicago Press, 2008.

Fisher, Janina. *Healing the Fragmented Selves of Trauma Survivors.* New York: Routledge, 2017.

Forster, Edward M. *Aspects of the Novel.* London and New York: Penguin. 1962.

Fox Michael V. The Meanings of the Book of Job. *Journal of Biblical Literature* 1 April 2018; 137 (1): 9. https://doi.org/10.15699/jbl.1371.2018.1372.

Frankl, Victor E. *Man's Search for Meaning,* 5th ed. Boston: Beacon Press, 2006.

Freeman, Mark. "Telling Stories: Memory and Narrative." In *Memory: Histories, Theories, Debates* 263–78. Fordham University Press, 2010. https://www.jstor.org/stable/j.ctt1c999bq.22. Accessed on Sat, 29 Jul 2023 00:45:49.

Frewen, Paul and Lanius, Ruth. *Healing the Traumatized Self.* New York: Norton, 2015.

Gaybba, Brian. *The Spirit of Love*. Geoffrey Chapman Theology Library, London, 1987.

Giddens, Anthony. 1991. Modernity and Self-Identity. Self and Society in the Late Modern Age. Stanford: Stanford University Press.1991.

Goldberg, Michael. *Theology and Narrative. A Critical Introduction.* Wipf and Stock Publishers, 2001.

Gordon, James S. *The Transformation: Discovering Wholeness and Healing after Trauma.* New York: HarperOne, 2019.

Gray, Robert. P. *Art Therapy and Psychology. A Step-by-Step Guide for Practitioners.* Routledge, 2019.

Grenz, Stanley J., and Roger Olson. *20ᵗʰ Century Theology: God & the World in a Transitional Age.* InterVarsity Press, 1992.

Grenz, Stanley J *Created for Community.* 3ʳᵈ ed. Baker Academic: Grand Rapids, 2014.

Haines, Staci, K., *The Politics of Trauma: Somatics, Healing and Social Justice.* Berkely: North Atlantic Books, 2019.

Hammer, Emanuel. *Clinical Application of Projective Drawings.* Springfield: (Charles C Thomas Publisher, Ltd, 1980). https://search-ebscohost-com.prov.idm.oclc.org/login.aspx?direct=true&db=nlebk&AN=476774&site=eho st-live.

Hauerwas, Stanley, and Gregory L. Eds. Jones. *Why Narrative? Readings In Narrative Theology.* Eugene. Oregon: Wipf and Stock Publishers, 1997.

Hatzikiriakidis Morris, H. K., Dwyer, J., Lewis, C., Halfpenny, N., Miller, R., & Skouteris, H. "Early Intervention for Residential Out-of-Home Care Staff Using Eye Movement Desensitization and Reprocessing (EMDR)." Psychological Trauma: Theory, Research, Practice, and Policy. 2022, assessed Sept 18, 2022, https://dx.doi.org/10.1037/tra0001418.

Heidegger, Martin "The Origin of the Work of Art." In *Poetry, Language, Thought*. New York: Harper and Row, 1975.

Henderson, Robert, *Operating in Courts of Heaven*. Shippensburg, PA: Destiny Image Publishers, 2021.

Herman, Judith. *Trauma and Recovery: The Aftermath of Violence - From Domestic Abuse to Political Terror*. New York: Basic Books, 2015.

Hildegard of Bingen. Ed. Star, M. *Devotions, Prayers and Living Wisdom*. Boulder: Sounds True, 2012.

Hogan, Susan. *Art Therapy Theories. A Critical Introduction*. Routledge, 2016.

Horan, Daniel P. *National Catholic Reporter*. 3/3/2023, Vol. 59 Issue 11.

Huebl, Thomas & Joubert, Kosha, in The Pocket Project, https://pocketproject.org.

Hyland Moon, C. *Materials and Media in Art Therapy. Critical Understanding of Diverse Artistic Vocabularies*. Routledge, Taylor and Francis Group, 2010.

Ismayilova, Leyla, Claypool, Emily and Heidorn, Emma. "Trauma of Separation: The Social and Emotional Impact of Institutionalization on Children in a Post-Soviet Country." *BMC Public Health* 23, no. 1 (February 20, 2023): 1–14. https://doi:10.1186/s12889-023-15275-w.

Jauss, Hans Robert and Shaw, Michael. "*Poiesis*" Critical Inquiry, Vol. 8, No. 3 (Spring, 1982), pp. 591- 608. Published by: The University of Chicago Press. Accessed on May 31, 2023. https://www.jstor.org/stable/1343267.

Kapic, Kelly, M. *A Little Book for New Theologians. Why and How to Study Theology*. InterVarsity Press Downers Grove, Il, 2012.

Kapitan, Lynne, *Introduction to Art Therapy Research*, 2nd ed. New York & London: Routledge, Taylor and Francis Group, 2018.

Katz, Judith, Noam Saadon, and Sharar Arzy. "The Life Review Experience: Qualitative and Quantitative Characteristics." *Consciousness and Cognition* Vol.48 (2017): 76–86, assessed Nov 10, 2022. https://doi-org.ezproxy.library.ubc.ca/10.1016/j.concog.2016.10.011.

Kepnes, Steven. *The Text as Thou: Martin Buber's Dialogical Hermeneutics and Narrative Theology.* Bloomington: Indiana University Press, 1992.

Kezelman, Cathy & Stavropoulos, Pam. *Practice Guidelines for Treatment of Complex Trauma and Trauma Informed Care and Service Delivery.* The Australian Government Department for Health and Aging. Blue Knot Foundation, 2017. https//blueknot.org.au.

Gerasimos & Olff, Miranda (2017) Psychotraumatology in Greece, European Journal of Psychotraumatology,8:sup.4. Accessed on May 12, 2023. https://www.tandfonline.com/doi/full/10.1080/20008198.2017.1351757.

Hildegard of Bingen: Ed. Star, *Devotions, Prayers & Living Wisdom.* Boulder: Sounds True Inc. 2008.

Larsen T, &. Treier. D.J., Eds. *The Cambridge Companion to Evangelical Theology.* (Cambridge University Press, 2007)

Levine, Peter. A., and Frederick, Ann. *Waking the Tiger. Healing Trauma. The Innate Capacity to Transform Overwhelming Experiences.* California: North Atlantic Books,1997.

Levine, Stephen. K. *Poiesis. The Language of Psychology and the Speech of the Soul.* 2nd ed. Canada: Palmerston Press, 1992.

---. *Trauma, Tragedy, Therapy. The Arts and Human Suffering.* London: Jessica Kingsley Publishers, 2009.

Leuzinger-Bohleber, Marianne. *Finding the Body in the Mind: Embodied Memories, Trauma, and Depression.* The International Psychoanalytical Association Psychoanalytic Ideas and Applications Series. London, United Kingdom: Routledge, 2015,

26 - 27. https://search-ebscohost- com.prov.idm.oclc.org/login. aspx?direct=true&db=nlebk&AN=1016526&site=eh ost- live.

Lewis, C.S., *Miracles. A Preliminary Study. Geoffrey Bles* The Centenary Press. London January 1, 1947.

Lobban, Janice and Taylor & Francis eBooks A-Z. *Art Therapy with Military Veterans: Trauma and the Image.* 1st;1; Vol. 1. New York, NY; Routledge, 2018. Assessed Nov 2022, https://doi. org/10.4324/9781315564197.

Macrì, Emanuela, and Costanzo Limoni. "Artistic Activities and Psychological Well-being Perceived by Patients with Spinal Cord Injury." *The Arts in Psychotherapy* 54 (July 1, 2017): 1–6, Accessed Sept 20, 2022, https://doi.org/10.1016/j.aip.2017.02.003.

Malchiodi, Cathy A. *Trauma and Expressive Arts Therapy. Brain, Body, & Imagination in the Healing Process.* The Guildford Press, 2020.

Maslow, Abraham Harold. *Motivation and Personality,* New York, Harper, 1954.

Maté, Gabor. "*On Compassionate Inquiry,*" assessed Feb.20, 2023, https:// medium.com/invisible-illness/trauma-expert-dr-gabor-mat% C3%A9-a42a6ce67726.

---. *When the Body Says No. Exploring the Stress-Disease Connection.* John Wiley & Sons, 2003.

McCloughen Isobel S.A, Goodyear M, Foster K. Intergenerational Trauma and Its Relationship to Mental Health Care: A Qualitative Inquiry. *Community Mental Health J.* 2021;57(4):631-643.Accessed May 31, 2022. https://doi:10.1007/s10597-020-00698-1.

McGrath, Alister E. *Narrative Apologetics: Sharing the Relevance, Joy, and Wonder of the Christian Faith.* Baker Books, 2019.

McGrath, A. E. ed. *The Christian Theology Reader.* 5th Edition. Chichester: Wiley Blackwell, 2016.

McGrath, A. E. *Christian Theology an Introduction,* 6th Ed. John Wiley & Sons Ltd. Oxford. U.K, 2017.

Meister, Jan Christoph and Schernus, Wilhelm. *Time: From Concept to Narrative Construct: A Reader.* Narratologia. Berlin: De Gruyter, 2011), 67. Accessed in June 2023. https://search-ebscohost- com.prov.idm. oclc.org/login.aspx?direct=true&db=nlebk&AN=390868&site=eho st-live.

McNiff, Shaun, *Trust the Process.* Shambhala, 1998.

Miller, Eric. "Story and Storytelling in Storytelling Therapy and Expressive Arts Therapy." *In Conference Proceedings.* International Expressive Arts Therapy Conference, Chennai (February 2017): 45–59.

Moon, B.L. Ph.D. *Art-Based Group Therapy. Theory and Practice.* Springfield. Illinois: Charles C Thomas, 2010.

Morris, H., Hatzikiriakidis, K., Dwyer, J., Lewis, C., Halfpenny, N., Miller, R., & Skouteris, H. (2022, December 22). Early Intervention for Residential Out-of- Home Care Staff Using Eye Movement Desensitization and Reprocessing (EMDR). Psychological Trauma: Theory, Research, Practice, and Policy, accessed December 22, 2022, https://dx.doi.org/10.1037/tra0001418.

Moustakas, Clark E. *Heuristic Research, Design, Methodology, and Applications.* Newbury Park, London: Sage Publications, 1990.

Najarian, Anie. *"Transmission of Trauma, Ritual, and Art Therapy,"* (Master Thesis) Concordia University. ProQuest Dissertations Publishing, 2007, assessed Nov. 19, 2022, https://www.routledge. com/Navigating-Art-Therapy-A-Therapists- Companion/Wood/p/ book/9780415223195.

Neethling, Kobus & Rutherford, Rache. *Am I clever or stupid?* NBI Publishing, 2004.

Newbigin, James E.L. *The Gospel in a Pluralist Society.* Grand Rapids: Eerdmans, 1989.

Niebuhr, Richard. *The Meaning of Revelation*. New York, MacMillan Publishing Company,1941.

Oxford English Dictionary. Ed. J. A. Simpson and E. S. C. Weiner. 2nd ed. Oxford: Clarendon Press, 1989. OED Online Oxford 23, 2007; cf. subliminal.

Palmisano, A. N., Meshberg-Cohen, S., Petrakis, I. L., & Sofuoglu, M. "A systematic review evaluating PTSD treatment effects on intermediate phenotypes of PTSD." *Psychological Trauma: Theory, Research, Practice, and Policy*. December 19, 2022: https://doi.org/10.1037/tra0001410.

Paintner,Christine Valters. *The Artist's Rule. A Twelve-week Journey. Nurturing your Creative Soul with Monastic Wisdom*. www.sorinbooks.com, 2011.

Pernicano, Pat. *Using Stories, Art and Play in Trauma-Informed Treatment: Case Examples and Applications across the Lifespan*. New York: Routledge, Taylor and Francis Group, 2019.

Perry, Bruce D and Winfrey, Oprah. *What Happened to You? Conversations on Trauma, Resilience, and Healing*. New York: Flatiron Books, 2021.

Peterson, Eugene, H. *Practice Resurrection: A Conversation on Growing Up in Christ*. Spiritual Theology #5: Eerdmans, 2010.

Pinnock, Clark H. A Review of Veli-Matti Käelieli-Matti Kärkkäinen's Pneumatology: The Holy Spirit in Ecumenical, International, and Contextual Perspective. Grand Rapids: Baker Academic, 2002.

Porges, Stephen. W., *The Pocket Guide to the Polyvagal Theory. The Transformative Power of Feeling Safe*. New York & London: W.W. Norton & Company, 2017.

Prior, R.W. ed. *Using Art as Research and Learning and Teaching. Multidisciplinary Approaches Across the Arts*. Intellect, 2018.

Puderbaugh M, Emmady PD. Neuroplasticity. 2022 May 8. In: StatPearls [Internet]. Treasure Island (FL): StatPearls Publishing; 2023 Jan–. PMID: 32491743

Rambo, Sally, *Spirit and Trauma: A Theology of Remaining.* Louisville, KY: Westminster John Knox, 2010.

Reed, Esther D., Freathy, Rob, Cornwall, Susanna and Davis, Anna. "Narrative Theology in Religious Education." *British Journal of Religious Education,* 2013 Vol. 35, No. 3, 298, http://dx.doi.org/10.1 080/01416200.2013.785931.

Richardson, Brian. "Recent Concepts of Narrative and the Narratives of Narrative Theory." Vol.34., no. 2. (Summer 2000): 168–175.

Ricoeur, Paul. *Oneself as Another Translated by Kathleen Blamey.* The University of Chicago Press. Chicago and London.1992.

Rubin, J.A. Editor. *Approaches to Art Therapy. Theory and Technique.* 3rd. Routledge, Taylor and Francis. 2016.

Schouten, Karin Alice, de Niet, Gerrit J., Knipscheer, Jeroen W., Kleber, Rolf, J. and Hutschemaekers, Giel., J. M. "The Effectiveness of Art Therapy in the Treatment of Traumatized Adults: A Systematic Review on Art Therapy and Trauma." *Trauma, Violence & Abuse* 16, no. 2 (2015): 220–28. https://doi.org/10.1177/1524838014555032.

Seiden, D. *Mind Over Matter: The Uses of Materials in Art, Education and Therapy.* Chicago: Magnolia Street. 2001.

Stephen, Darryl. "A Trauma-Informed Approach to Christian Ethics," *Journal of Feminist Studies in Religion (Indiana University Press* 39, no. 1 (March 1, 2023): 155–174.

Strong, James, *Strong's Exhaustive Concordance* Hendrickson Publishers, 2009.

Townsend, Tamara L. *Memory and Identity in the Narratives of Soledad Puértolas: Constructing the Past and the Self.* Lanham, Maryland: Lexington Books, 2014. https://search-ebscohost- com.prov.idm.

oclc.org/login.aspx?direct=true&db=nlebk&AN=846022&site=eho st-live.

Tutu, Desmond, W. *No Future Without Forgiveness*. 2nd.ed. London: Random House. 2000.

Van Der Kolk, Bessel. *The Body Keeps Score: Brain, Mind, and Body in the Healing of Trauma*. Penguin Books, 2015.

Van Der Kolk, et al. "Pain Perception and Endogenous Opioids in Post Traumatic Stress Disorder," *Psychopharmacology Bulletin 25* (1989), 117 -121.

Van Deusen Hunsinger, Deborah. *Bearing the Unbearable. Trauma, Gospel, and Pastoral Care*. Grand Rapids, Michigan: William B Eerdmans Publishers Company, 2015.

Wadeson, H. *Art Therapy Practice: Innovative Approaches with Diverse Populations. New York: Wiley & Sons*. 2000.

Weisskopf, Edith. The Place of Logotherapy in the World Today." *The International Forum for Logotherapy, Vol.1. No3. (1980)*.

Wexler, Bruce E. *Brain, and Culture: Neurobiology, Ideology, and Social Change*. (Cambridge, Mass: Bradford Books, 2006. https://search-ebscohost- com.prov.idm.oclc.org/login.aspx?direct=true&db= nlebk&AN=156966&site=eho st-live.

Wilkinson, Rebecca A., & Chilton, Gioia. "Positive Art Therapy: Linking Positive Psychology to Art Therapy Theory, Practice, and Research." *Art Therapy* 30, no. 1 (January 1, 2013): 4–11, assessed October 10, 2022. https://doi.org/10.1080/07421656.2013.757513.

Wong, Paul T.P. "The Processes of Adaptive Reminiscence," in *The Art and Science of Reminiscing: Theory, Research, Methods, and Applications* (Washington, D.C, Taylor and Francis, 1995.

Wood, C. Ed. *Navigating Art Therapy. A Therapist's Companion*. Routledge, 2011.

Wood, David. *On Paul Ricoeur: Narrative and Interpretation.* London: Routledge, 1991.

Wu, Yue Kris, Friedemann, Zenke. How Neurons That Wire Together Fire Together. Dec 23, 2021. https://neurosciencenews.com/wire-fire-neurons-19835/ (2021) Nonlinear transient amplification in recurrent neural networks with short-term plasticity eLife 10:e71263.

Young, Edward J., *An Introduction to the Old Testament.* Grand Rapids, Michigan: William Eerdmans Publishing Co. 1978.